For Karen

The Death of the Good Canadian

Studies in the
Postmodern Theory of Education

Joe L. Kincheloe and Shirley R. Steinberg
General Editors

Vol. 197

PETER LANG
New York • Washington, D.C./Baltimore • Bern
Frankfurt am Main • Berlin • Brussels • Vienna • Oxford

George H. Richardson

The Death of the Good Canadian

Teachers, National Identities,
and the Social Studies Curriculum

PETER LANG
New York • Washington, D.C./Baltimore • Bern
Frankfurt am Main • Berlin • Brussels • Vienna • Oxford

Library of Congress Cataloging-in-Publication Data

Richardson, George H.
The death of the good Canadian: teachers, national identities,
and the social studies curriculum / George H. Richardson.
p. cm. — (Counterpoints; vol. 197)
Includes bibliographical references (p.   ) and index.
1. Social sciences—Study and teaching—Canada. 2. Postmodernism
and education—Canada. 3. National characteristics, Canadian.
I. Title. II. Counterpoints (New York, N.Y.); vol. 197.
LB1584.5.C2 R53   300'.71'071—dc21   2001029118
ISBN 0-8204-5535-0
ISSN 1058-1634

Die Deutsche Bibliothek-CIP-Einheitsaufnahme

Richardson, George H.:
The death of the good Canadian: teachers, national identities,
and the social studies curriculum / George H. Richardson.
–New York; Washington, D.C./Baltimore; Bern;
Frankfurt am Main; Berlin; Brussels; Vienna; Oxford: Lang.
(Counterpoints; Vol. 197)
ISBN 0-8204-5535-0

Cover design by Joni Holst

The paper in this book meets the guidelines for permanence and durability
of the Committee on Production Guidelines for Book Longevity
of the Council of Library Resources.

© 2002 Peter Lang Publishing, Inc., New York

Printed in the United States of America

TABLE OF CONTENTS

ACKNOWLEDGMENTS

I would like to thank the teachers who took part in this project. Their enthusiastic commitment to the idea that it was possible for teachers to collectively reconceptualize the teaching of national identity was the force that continually drove the research. In an era when teaching is undervalued and teachers themselves are increasingly constrained by the dictates of narrowly conceived, market driven, outcomes-based education, the dedication my teaching colleagues showed to the research stands as powerful evidence of the creativity and passion teachers bring to the teaching profession. I would also like to thank my colleagues in the Department of Secondary Education at the University of Alberta for the help and useful advice they have given me during my short tenure in the Department. Specifically, I would like to express my gratitude to Terry Carson, Ingrid Johnston, jan jagodzinski, David G. Smith, and David Blades for their continuing encouragement and support in this project and in other endeavors. Finally, I want to thank my family for their patience and love.

CHAPTER 1
The Subtle Geography of the Interrogative

C'est très difficile de <<s'expliquer>>—une interview, un dialogue, un entretien. La plupart du temps, quand on me pose une question, même qui me touche, je m'aperçois que je n'ai strictement rien à dire.
—Deleuze and Parnet, *Dialogues*

Introduction: The Problem Position

Deleuze and Parnet's observations about the difficulty of explaining oneself in the public sphere represents, I think, an acknowledgment of the complexity, ambiguity, and multilayered nature of human discourse. Increasingly, when faced with the question of education or the question of the curriculum, or the question of teaching, like Deleuze and Parnet, I too find that I don't have much to say.

At issue here is not the relevance of the particular questions posed, nor is it a question of whether everything has already been said in the realm of educational discourse. Rather, it is the question of the question itself. The problem of what we mean when we ask questions and what answers those questions elicit emerged many times during the course of my research. But one incident from that period stands out: At the conclusion of my research, a colleague on the faculty interviewed me about my views on education and national identity formation, the topic that is the focus of this book. In the course of the interview, I found myself answering yes to most of the questions that were put to me: Did I believe that individual identity and ethnic or group identity had a major impact on the formation of national identity? Yes. Did I think that the curriculum should acknowledge this relationship? Yes. Was national identity formation in plural societies as much a matter of acknowledgment of difference as it was a celebration of commonality and should the curriculum represent both these forces? Again, yes. Later, as I read over the text of the interview, it struck me how little we had actually discussed and how the questions themselves had glossed over the subtle and complex substrata of intellectual, emotional, and psychological processes that had been distilled into my responses.

A famous Jules Pfeiffer cartoon in the *New Yorker* raises the same issue of the problematic nature of fixing meaning around what appear to be even the most commonplace loci of certainty. Two men meeting each other in the street exchange their customary greeting: "How are you," one asks. "Fine." is the response. But the man to whom the question was put asks himself after the fact: "Exactly what did he mean by that?" (*New Yorker* 1975) From a poststructuralist stance, such direct questions are unanswerable because they essentialize meaning and narrowly frame the range of possible responses (Barthes 1988; Ducrot 1984). Deleuze and Parnet (1977) suggest that rather than questions, we should think in terms of "problem positions." Such positions are shifting locations composed of a complex series of emotional and intellectual strands (Deleuze and Parnet use the term *tracé*). These strands never group together to establish absolute meaning; rather, they represent the geomorphology of the problematic, they situate the individual within a more fluid terrain of meaning that they call *le tracé d'un devenir*[1] (p. 8). Describing this terrain, they write *c'est de la géographie, ce sont des orientations, des directions, des entrées et des sortis* (ibid.).

To anyone with experience in classroom teaching, and certainly to those engaged in teaching social studies, the notions of the complexity, ambiguity, and flux that lie at the heart of Deleuze and Parnet's observations about human interactions are particularly appropriate. Curriculum scholar T. T. Aoki, for example, notes both the "in-betweeness" that characterizes the lives of classroom teachers and the "multilayered voices" that represent the "reality" of teaching (1992). But such a location should not be confused with the average or the mean, nor should it be considered as some neutral meeting ground between teachers and students or between the curriculum and the classroom. It is rather the place where the strands of problem positions cross and recross, a site that Deleuze and Parnet define as *les noces entre deux règnes* (Deleuze and Parnet 1977, 8).

In many ways, this book takes up the strands of identity tied to the problem positions that emerge from the complex location teachers occupy. Caught in the rough ground between the curriculum as authoritative text and the lived curriculum of the classroom and between static modernist constructions of national identity and their own, more fluid, identities, teachers find that they don't have much to say when faced with the question of education. Because this lack of response is too often misread as disengagement or withdrawal, I attempt to explore the geography of teaching at a time when the pedagogical terrain is shifting rapidly. Although its focus is on national identity, this book is as much about the individual identity of teachers as it is about the role of the curriculum in creating what Benedict Anderson has called a "common imagining" of the nation (Anderson 1995).

Le Tracé d'un Devenir

During my own career as a classroom teacher, I have come to question the notion that there are answers to the questions that education poses. In the face of such questions as "What do you think students should learn?" "How do you think they should be taught?" "What role do you think teachers should play in education?" my response has become strikingly similar to the reaction Deleuze and Parnet describe—I don't have much to say. Such questions leave no space for the problem position; they solicit instead a kind of finality that closes all discourse (Jardine 1992). Like Deleuze and Parnet, I see the geography of the interrogative as more shifting and fluid. Hans-Georg Gadamer captured this well when he wrote, "the openness of what is in question consists of the fact that the answer is not settled" (1975, 326).

But appreciation for "the openness of what is in question" was no startling epiphany on my part. It began with the culture shock that is typical of the first years of any teacher's career and has continued in the gradual and occasionally painful process of learning that education, in Donald Schon's (1991) brilliantly human description, is taken up mainly with "managing messes."

As a beginning teacher in a remote northern community in the 1970s, who was teaching a social studies program that posed the question of poverty in Canada in essentially urban and culturally Anglo Saxon terms, I was faced with the ironic fact that many of my Metis and Aboriginal students lived in a world that was equally poverty stricken. However, this world remained all but invisible because it was neither described in the curriculum nor was it present in the resources we used. Although this invisibility was a concern to me, as a young teacher eager to engage my students in the values clarification and social inquiry approaches that were then sweeping through the social studies, I continued to teach the curriculum to the best of my abilities. But despite the broadly liberal and reconstructionist thrust of social studies, my students were frankly bored with it. Reflecting on this boredom later, I came to the conclusion that their reaction was a logical response to their own marginalization. Why should they enter into a dialogue with a curriculum that refused to acknowledge their existence?

The growing conviction that there was a reproductionist agenda (Bourdieu and Passeron 1977; Apple, 1978) underlying the curriculum, aimed at legitimating existing social and economic structures at the expense of other perspectives (those of women, aboriginal Canadians and ethnocultural minorities), was reinforced by my long-term involvement in the design and production of compulsory province-wide social studies examinations. What was mandated in the provincial curriculum was what we tested, but increasingly the examination assumed the form of an unanswerable question for students and the response it elicited was similar to the reaction Deleuze and Parnet describe: silence and acquiescence.

As the emphasis on high stakes testing continued into the 1990s and the structure of examinations increasingly dictated the curriculum, I began to notice that my students became less interested in the course itself and more anxious about the exam. This particularly postmodern combination of apathy and anxiety (Borgmann 1992) was most evident in the young women in my social studies classes. For some time it had been quite clear to me that women generally found the social studies curriculum—with its heavy emphasis on power politics and military conflict and the virtual absence of portrayals of females—alienating, but when combined with the pressure that a mandatory examination brought to the course, many of my female students expressed a resentment toward social studies that was striking in its intensity.

If the gradual realization that the curriculum represented a closed set of historical and cultural referents, and that the prescriptive nature of most programs of studies effectively excluded and delegitimized the histories of others who were not named (Kanpol and McLaren 1995) brought me to question the legitimacy of the content of the *Program of Studies*, a six-month teaching assignment in Ukraine in 1993 led me to question the appropriateness of social studies methods that frame critical social and political issues in a kind of culturally decontextualized interrogative.

Tentative Steps Toward a Problem Position

In 1993, Ukraine was in the process of a massive social, economic, and political transformation. The scope of this change in Ukraine and in other states that formerly comprised the Soviet Union was and remains today immense and problematic. It involved at one and the same time the attempt to introduce a partial market economy, create democratic political structures and an independent judiciary, rebuild the economic infrastructure, and modernize the education system. In itself this task was daunting enough; but even more intimidating was the need to develop an ideology and a system of values that were essential if the structural changes were to survive.

Teaching in this environment was both exciting and intimidating. Yet in many respects, the experience was also surprisingly similar to teaching in Canada. In terms of the overt form and function of teaching, there were classrooms, age and grade groupings, texts, homework, examinations, and questions of classroom management and a host of related issues that would be immediately familiar to any teacher. But what was entirely different was the cultural and political context in which education took place.

This difference in context had two significant consequences for me. It brought me to question the cultural assumptions I had made about my discipline, and, ultimately, it brought me to the problem position that this book speaks from.

My experience as a classroom teacher had led me to the conclusion that there was a dominant metanarrative (after Lyotard 1993) in the content of programs of studies that acted to privilege a particular understanding of society and, by extension, exclude and delegitimate all competing or alternate views (Apple 1993; Giroux 1993a), but I had always assumed that the techniques of social studies—in particular the inquiry method with its cycle of fact-finding, generalization forming, evaluation, and action—(Government of Alberta 1990) were value neutral and were, in fact, essential for social progress and the production of responsible citizens.

But events in Russia in October 1993 caused me to question these assumptions. The abortive coup that month, in which old-line communists in the Russian Duma, backed by elements of the Russian army, attempted to seize control of all television and radio stations in Moscow was broadcast live in Ukraine as well as in Russia. The images of pitched gun battles filmed on-the-spot and reported live by nervous Russian newscasters struck me as a wonderful opportunity to ask my students important questions about issues of power, democracy, and freedom of expression within newly independent nations struggling to establish more open political structures.

However, when I asked them to comment on the crisis and to indicate and explain their position on the events (were they for or against the coup and why), I was met with stubborn silence on their part, and I met the same reaction from my teaching colleagues in the school. My initial conclusions about this lack of response were as stereotypical as they were wrong. Years of communist domination had removed or suppressed the capacity to think critically. They could no longer ask nor answer the *hard* questions, I concluded, and it was my task to develop this ability.

It was only some weeks later, when the crisis had died down and it was clear Boris Yeltsin and the reformists had won the day that my students and colleagues firmly but gently pointed out the mistakes I had made in demanding that they *think critically*. Had the old-line forces won, many Ukrainians feared a return to communist domination. In that event, any criticism of the new regime (even in the relatively benign context of a classroom discussion) could be dangerous. Far from refusing to think critically, then, my students and colleagues had made a very sophisticated analysis of the political situation and had acted in accordance with their conclusions. What for me had been a teachable moment in the development of the inquiry method was for them an irresponsible and frankly dangerous exercise in which they might have found themselves and their families exposed to persecution.

Establishing a Geography of Relations

The idea that there was a whole series of cultural assumptions underlying Canadian social studies methodologies that were not easily transferable to other cultural contexts led me back to the *question of the question* and, eventually to the notion, basic to Deleuze, Parnet, Gadamer, Jardine and others, that the question must somehow assume a more open form that allowed for an understanding of the complexities of the issue at hand rather than precluding discussion. And if the question was to function in this way and be open to the many strands that would inevitably cross and recross, it could not be put in direct terms. Ideally it would emerge as a problem position that reflected the varied experiences and perceptions of the participants in such a way that a "géographie des relations" (Deleuze and Parnet, 1977, 70) developed.

In my case the issue that emerged during my time in Ukraine was how nationalism and national identity (both essentially 19th century concepts) are formed and sustained in an era when nations are becoming more plural and when nationalism itself is in competition with globalization (Kymlicka, 1995; Barber, 1995).

Watching the attempt of the Ukrainian State to manufacture an identity that fit the economic and political conditions of the 1990s while at the same time maintaining traditional Ukrainian culture, I was struck by the strong parallels with the Canadian experience. Similarly to Ukrainian identity, Canadian identity had had to cope with the impact of political, economic and cultural colonization, and comparable to Ukraine, education was considered to be a critical factor in the development and maintenance of national identity. Clearly, in the case of Ukraine, the difficulties involved in the attempt to foster and protect a national identity were far greater than those Canadians had ever had to face, but it was the process rather than the conditions under which the process took place that seemed markedly similar to me.

I returned from Ukraine and presented a series of workshops and professional development sessions on my experience of education and society in the post-Soviet period, but in the course of those sessions, I was almost always invited to express my views on nationalism in the post-Cold War era. At the time much was being made in the media about the death of communism and the rise of nationalism in its place. And nationalism itself, or at least ethnic nationalism, was generally presented in negative terms as a dangerous precursor to intolerance and violence.[2]

Because I had been *on the scene,* it was assumed that I had some form of expert knowledge about nationalism as a post-Cold War phenomenon, an assumption that was very much unwarranted. But the invitation provided me with an opportunity to explore nationalism from a different perspective. I proposed to four social studies teachers, with whom I had taught for many years, that collectively we take up the issue of how we conceived of nationalism in the post-Cold War period. Like Deleuze and Parnet, I had no answer to the question of what I thought of the phenomenon of renascent nationalism, but I was interested in engaging in a "geography of relations" that opened up the question of teachers' perceptions of nationalism, and in particular of how they viewed the portrayal of nationalism in the curriculum.

Conclusion

What emerged from this collective conversation about nationalism was a problem position focusing on how the social studies curriculum represents national identity and in which the strands of national and personal identity, perceptions about teaching and students, differing views about the curriculum and the ends of education constantly interwove.   A key result of these discussions was the emergent understanding that ambiguity and uncertainty appear to characterize both our perceptions of national identity and our understanding of our role as teachers.

In search of a set of theoretical frameworks that would allow me to engage in Deleuze's "geography of relations" with my teaching colleagues, I turned to action research informed by postmodernism and hermeneutics. In Chapter 2, I examine these research orientations and how they apply to the study of education and national identity.

CHAPTER 2
Spelunking in Hell: Theory into Practice

Look, this is really hard stuff for me. I thought I knew my kids and the curriculum, but now you're telling me that this whole section on Identity doesn't mean anything. If it doesn't really matter, then why should I care? What would be the point?

—John

Avant propos

John's complaint, voiced midway through the action research project, was more than an expression of frustration at having to grapple with the abstractions of postmodern educational thought and the difficulties of reflecting on his own educational practice. It was, I think, a genuine expression of his desire to understand what it means to teach given the ambiguity that characterizes the life of classroom teachers. More importantly, it was an expression of a fundamental ethical problem that lies at the core of contemporary education. That question revolves around the issue of what right action is in the face of what David G. Smith refers to as the "immobilizing tension between the [Enlightenment] myth of coherence and the truth of its disintegration" (1995, 19). As I searched for an adequate response to this issue, it was necessary to turn to scholarly writings in postmodernism, hermeneutics, and action research. But as a classroom teacher, long inured to focusing on the practice of teaching, this venture into the field of theory was both intimidating and humbling. The title of Chapter 2 reflects the difficulties I faced; I still recall the response of one of my students when I attempted to describe to her what it was I was doing at university. "Geez, Mr. R.," she said, "that sounds pretty intense." It was.

Introduction

Together, hermeneutics, postmodernism, and action research effectively create a site somewhere between the dictates of the curriculum and the lived world of the classroom, where, in Terry Carson's words, "a space for ethical reflection is now opened between theory and practice" (1992, 14). But in order to delineate the parameters of that reflective space, it is important to examine how each research orientation approaches national identity and education.

Part I: Postmodernism

> The postmodern reply to the modern consists of recognizing that the past, since it cannot really be destroyed, because its destruction leads to silence, must be revisited: but with irony and not innocently. (Eco, 1983, postscript)

The terrain of postmodernism is varied and extensive. Touching fields as diverse as semiotics, literary theory, architecture, popular culture, radical politics, philosophy, and educational thought, postmodernism has been seen as both a designation of a particular period in history and as a critique or a mode of analysis of modernism (Harvey 1989; Jameson 1991). Furthermore, it is much-contested ground. Its proponents see in postmodernism's problematization of objectivity, language, and meaning a kind of emancipatory thrust that *frees up* space for the voices of *others* typically silenced by modernism (Greene 1997). Yet its critics see in this same problematization a dangerous nihilism that encourages a kind of intellectual stasis that diminishes the possibility of solidarity and genuine social change (Sloterdijk 1987; Eagleton 1996). It is not the purpose of this book to engage in this debate, but I will argue that in terms of its potential impact on education, postmodernism carries with it ambiguous possibilities.

It is impossible to discuss postmodernism as a unified philosophical system. If there is any salient characteristic of postmodernism, it is its rejection of the totalizing effects of what Jean-Francois Lyotard (1993) termed "metanarratives." Thus, postmodernism is not easily defined, and from a postmodern perspective, the act of definition itself is problematic. Delimiting the essential qualities of any idea or object closes the door to other possible meanings and, as Jacques Lacan suggests, the act of *naming* a thing is a way of killing it.

> The word is a death, a murder of a thing: as soon as the reality is symbolized, caught in a symbolic network, the thing itself is more present in a word, in its concept than in its immediate physical reality. (Lacan in Zizek 1989, 131)

A further complication in attempting to describe postmodernism is that postmodernist thought emphasizes that the relationship of language to meaning is equally problematic. Postmodern writers tend to reject the neutral view that language is a universal and transparent medium for transmitting ideas and meaning (Derrida 1993; Foucault 1972; Lacan 1977). Instead, postmodernists generally see language as something that reflects both the presuppositions and cultural assumptions of its traditions. Thus in Deborah Britzman's terms, "Meaning becomes the site of departure, a place where reality is constructed, truth is produced and power is effected" (1991, 25). That language is both contingent and contextual leads to the conclusion that the meaning of anything is at best problematic, and that meaning is "never knowable purely in and of itself, but only so far as it bears a relationship to something or to others" (D. Smith 1989, 6).

Although postmodernism is inherently resistant to definition in a formal sense, it is nevertheless possible to sketch some general characteristics of the movement. The characteristics that I outline below have particular significance for classroom teachers for critical instrumental reasons. Postmodernism's attack on the canon of modernism, its emphasis on the uncertainty and ambivalence that characterize all human relationships, its problematization of autonomous identities, and its valorization of the unheard voices of *others* submerged in the metanarrative of nationalism and national identity provide teachers with the analytical tools that are a necessary precondition to examining their own perceptions and practices and for formulating a curriculum that has more relevance for their students and for themselves.

Postmodernism as a Reaction against Modernism

In David Ray Griffin's terms, postmodernism is first and foremost a reaction to modernism founded on "a diffuse sentiment rather than to any set of common doctrines—the sentiment that humanity can and must go beyond the modern" (1993, vii–viii). An essential first step to going "beyond the modern" is a thorough examination of modernism itself. In particular, this interrogation of modernity has led postmodernists to a critical examination of Enlightenment culture and its attendant notions of progress, reason, control, and optimism leading to the conclusion of Gary Peller that:

> [postmodernism] suggests that what has been presented in our socio-political and our intellectual traditions as knowledge, truth, objectivity, and reason are actually merely the effects of a particular form of social power, the victory of

a particular way of representing the world that then presents itself as beyond interpretation, as truth itself. (1987, 30)

Postmodernism as an Acknowledgment of Ambivalence

Perhaps in reaction to the sense of certainty that emerged out of the modernist perspective that poses an autonomous subject capable of independent action who possess the tools (knowledge, reason, science) to allow for control over nature, postmodernism acknowledges the ambivalence and uncertainty that seem to be part of the lived experiences of life. For Jane Flax, this ambivalence is a "necessary ambivalence" resulting from the disjunction between experience and the socially constructed norms that govern our lives (1990, 9). And Patti Lather notes that postmodernism reveals the "profound uncertainty about what constitutes an adequate description of social reality" (1991, 21).

Postmodernism as a Challenge to the Autonomous Subject

Related to the challenge postmodernism poses to the modernist notion of certainty is its rejection of the concept that the identity of the subject is autonomous and independent. In modernist terms, identity is first and foremost associated with sovereignty and control (Fitzgerald 1993). Charles Taylor, for example, refers to the "autonomy [and] fulfillment of our nature and efficacy" that mark the chief characteristics of modernism, all of which represent a "confirmation of our control" (1993, 74). Albert Borgmann writes of modernist identity in terms of its celebration of "the unencumbered and autonomous human being" (1992, 25).

In postmodernism, however, the modernist Cartesian binary that allowed the subject to separate itself from the object is entirely ruptured and identity must be understood as relational (D. Smith 1989). The subject is always understood as the subject in context (Fitzgerald 1993). Thus, narratives outside ourselves "significantly contribute to the material from which our own narratives are derived" (Kerby 1991, 5–6). But in postmodern terms, the relational nature of identity is deeply political (Heller 1993) and implies both negotiation and an acknowledgment of relationships of power and difference that underlie all human interactions. In a postmodern sense, then, the subject is constituted through practices of subjection, or...through practices of liberation, of freedom...starting of course from a certain number of rules, styles and conventions that are found in culture. (Foucault, 1989, 313)

However, the "rules, styles and conventions" that Foucault refers to are not simply the cultural superstructure against which the individual must pose his or her own identity. In postmodernism, identity is not formed in the clash of Marxist dialectics; rather, identity is more commonly viewed as a process of negotiation between "individual subjectivities" and "objective cultural identity" (Balibar 1995, 174). The implication of Balibar's conclusions is that identity is both hybrid and fluid. This theme of the hybridity and mutability of identity is reinforced by Joan Scott who notes that identity is "the unstable, never-secured effect of a process of enunciation of cultural difference" (1995, 11). The same refusal to view identity formation in fixed terms can be drawn from the work of Richard Rorty, who describes the human self as "a network of beliefs, desires and emotions with nothing behind it constantly reweaving itself not by reference to general criteria but in the hit-or-miss way in which cells readjust themselves to meet pressures from the environment" (Rorty 1989, 217).

Just as individual identity is a process of negotiation rather than an acquisition of objective characteristics, group or national identity, viewed from a postmodern stance, is also continually in flux. Even critics of postmodernism acknowledge the impossibility of fixed concepts of national identity. For example, Thomas Fitzgerald, while expressing serious reservations about what he terms the postmodern tendency to confuse changing metaphors of identity with a change in the function of identity itself (1993, 53–54), notes that the formation of national identity is very much a deliberate act representing "not revitalization of static past traditions, but the conscious discovery of...common interest" (p. 190). And Fitzgerald further acknowledges the tension and ambivalence inherent in the disjunction he notes between "dramatic exhibitions of identities based on ethnic/gender/sexual preference" and "more and more media-influenced cultural homogenization of American [read Western] societies" (p. 195).

Postmodernist writers themselves tend to see the concepts of *nation* and *national identity* as Western constructs more associated with patterns of dominance and assimilation than with Benedict Anderson's notion of "common imagining" (Said 1994; Laclau 1995). But if the metanarrative of national identity itself is rejected, its significance is not. Postmodern writers discuss national identity in terms that emphasize the themes of hybridity, change and power relationships mentioned above. Thus for postcolonial theorist, Homi Bhabha, the idea of nation is, at best, an ambivalent concept bound up in "its transitional history [and] its conceptual indeterminacy..." (1990a, 307) but as an intellectual *location* it has critical importance as a site of interaction between the dominant culture and those subordinate cultures it seeks to assimilate (p. 309).

This site Bhabha has named the "third space," and, as is the case in the postmodern view of individual identity, it is a location of negotiation and hybridity:

> All forms of culture are constantly in a process of hybridity —this 3rd space between two originary moments displaces the histories that constitute it, and sets up new structures of authority, new political initiatives, which are inadequately understood through received wisdom. (1990b, 211)

But in a postmodern sense, negotiation and hybridity should not be confused with liberal notions of consensus and compromise. The "process of enunciation of cultural difference" that Scott (1995, 11) notes makes it, in Bhabha's terms, "very difficult, even impossible and counterproductive, to try and fit together different forms of culture and to pretend that they can easily coexist" (1990b, 210). Postmodernism, then, asserts the challenging notion that the "dense particularities" specific to each group making up the nation reforms and dislocates the intellectual geography of national identity in such a way that "we see ourselves as living—and having lived—in entirely heterogeneous and discrete places" (S. P. Mohanty, 1989, 13).

If postmodernism refuses to accept the overdetermination implicit in the nineteenth-century idea of "the nation", it nevertheless suggests more open alternatives to the current formulation of national identity. Thus, while Mohanty can point out how problematic national identity is in plural states, he can also suggest that a less restricting and restrictive approach to national identity might be to examine how the difference and conflict that lie at the center of the historical experience of all groups is essentially a shared experience (1989, 13).[1]

In postmodern writing, the idea of difference, in particular, has been identified as a critical source of national identity. For example, both Edward Said and Homi Bhabha stress that Western national identity emerges from a binary relationship that requires the presence of a non-

Western "other" for complete realization (Said 1979; Bhabha 1990b). And although some observers (Kristeva 1993; Salecl 1994) see the process of othering as a dangerous precursor to xenophobia and violence, others such as Stuart Hall have shown that "the internalization of the self-as-other" (1991, 256) has created (especially for the West) an open and constantly shifting boundary between West and non-West in which "America leads to Africa; the nations of Europe and Asia meet in Australia; the margins of history displace the center; the peoples of the periphery return to rewrite the history and fiction of the metropolis" (Bhabha 1990b, 312).

The idea that national identity represents a series of permeable and continually transgressed borders between self and other, between nation and foreign, effectively opens up a locus of negotiation that Gyatri Spivak refers to as a "decolonized space" (1987, 259) in which the experience of both halves of the binary must be acknowledged. At the heart of that acknowledgment lies an acceptance that we are all "others" and that difference and conflict are the common experience we all share. And in that opening up we move back to Gary Peller's (1987) insistence that postmodernism reveals the existence of other truths that lie outside the dominant discourse realm of modernism.

Thus it could be said that, in terms of national identity, postmodernism attempts to illuminate the "as yet unreadable alternative history" (Spivak 1987, 259) that constitutes the lived experience of marginalized cultures. In this light Ernesto Laclau notes that one particularly hopeful consequence of the destruction of the privileged position of the Enlightenment metanarrative will be the "proliferation of discursive interventions and arguments that become the source of greater activism and a more radical libertarianism" (1988, 79–80). And while expressing reservations about the inability of postmodernism to initiate genuine social transformation, David Harvey concludes that one of postmodernism's greatest contributions has been in acknowledging "the multiple forms of otherness as they emerge from differences in subjectivity, gender and sexuality, race and class, temporal (configurations of sensibility) and spatial geographic locations and dislocations" (1989, 113).

The postmodernist opposition to the exclusive nature of the myth of national foundations and its resultant emphasis on the need to attend to multiple narratives of existence has profound implications for education and for the teaching of national identity in Canadian schools. Using the tools postmodernism provides, it is possible to sketch the general outline of what a postmodern curriculum might look like and to begin to formulate an alternative and more democratic narrative of national identity.

Postmodernist Education

In some senses postmodernism, with its emphasis on multiplicity and its rejection of theoretical constructs that propose universally understood narratives in favor of the concrete and the local, appears ideally suited to the classrooms of the late twentieth century. Ethnically plural and culturally diverse, these classrooms seem to offer the possibility of opening up the question of what national identity means in plural cultures. But the changing ethnic and cultural map of the classroom presents complex choices to both curriculum designers and teachers alike. On the one hand, it is possible to attempt to impose a modernist and fairly rigid pedagogical infrastructure (curricula, texts, teaching styles) predicated on the existence of a common cultural understanding or with the aim of assimilating others to the common culture. However, given widespread dispute over which "common imagining" Canadian identity represents,[1] this attempt seems problematic at best.

On the other hand, postmodernism, in its reluctance to theorize a "better world," leaves classroom educators uncomfortably aware of the internal contradictions of the modernist approach to national identity yet without strategies or approaches to begin to work toward elaborating a more open formulation of national identity. The net result of this awareness may be a kind of intellectual and moral stasis that leads toward a helpless acceptance of the status quo (Giroux 1991, 20). At the very least, the postmodern delegitimization of certainty has left educators with an absurdist dilemma that David G. Smith captures quite well: how to proceed "after we have given up the presumption of ever being able to define in unequivocal terms all of the key referents in our professional lexicon" (1991, 188). This tendency of postmodernism to concern itself more with aesthetics than with praxis (Beyer and Liston 1996, 152–53) remains a significant problem for those attempting to incorporate postmodern understandings within educational environments.

The Characteristics of Postmodern Education

With this critical caveat in mind, it is nevertheless possible to attempt to describe what postmodern education might look like. For Clive Beck, the critique postmodernism directs at modernism represents an opportunity to introduce a more dialogic and democratic approach to education, one in which "teachers and students [learn] together, rather than the one telling the other how to live" (1997, 8). In *Curriculum Development in the Postmodern Era,* Patrick Slattery expands on the emancipatory possibilities postmodernism brings to education and suggests that a postmodern curriculum has five key elements:

1. It "respects the unique development of the individual and recognizes the interrelationship of all experiences."
2. It "must be formed in classrooms where the discourse is shared, empowering, emerging and tentative."
3. It "is eclectic and kaleidoscopic, and...should move beyond the oppressive structures of modernity."
4. It must be viewed in terms of the process of enlightenment rather than in terms of specific educational ends.
5. It must be inclusive and must draw from a variety of contemporary theories. (1995, 353–55)

Slattery's vision of a postmodern curriculum that accentuates personal experience, inclusion, and social transformation is echoed in the writings of Thomas Skrtic's work on special education. Arguing against the metanarrative of disability and for a more open understanding of the multiple narratives of the differently abled, Skrtic frames a definition of postmodern schooling that matches the social reconstructionist standpoint of Slattery and Beck while at the same time suggesting a tentative postmodern methodology:

> The curriculum and pedagogy in these [postmodern] schools will promote students' sense of social responsibility, awareness of interdependence, and appreciation of uncertainty by cultivating their capacity for experiential learning through collaborative problem solving and reflective discourse within a democratic community of interests. (1995, 259)

Henry Giroux adopts a reconstructionist position similar to that of Slattery and Skrtic, but moves beyond the tentative moral stance that is implicit in Slattery's criticism of modernism. Discussing what he refers to as "emancipatory postmodernism," Giroux notes that postmodernist "knowledge communities [must] answer for their choices even as these choices are provisional and viewed skeptically and even ironically" (1991, 19). Giroux's refusal to abandon the moral ground that is implied by postmodernism's reluctance to move beyond critique is predicated on a reconstructionist attempt to bridge the gap between social criticism and social change. But this stance implies a form of praxis that suggests a return to the kind of theorizing that is the very antithesis of postmodernism. The dilemma this represents is partly resolved by Barry Kanpol and Peter McLaren.

Writing in *Critical Multiculturalism: Uncommon Voices in a Common Struggle*, they stress the need for critical pedagogy to reformulate "the role of historical agency in the postmodern era," but warn that critical pedagogy must "avoid becoming yet another master narrative or essentialist form of truth construction" (1995, 5). Although Kanpol and McLaren leave unanswered the crucial question of how critical pedagogy can, in fact, avoid the temptation to substitute one master signifier for another, the fact that they acknowledge the dangers inherent in their approach ties them to the contingency Henry Giroux expresses when he writes of the skepticism and irony that are necessary preconditions for assuming agency in the postmodern world.

Postmodernism's distrust of theory appears to represent an obstacle to those (Giroux, Slattery, McLaren, Kanpol, Aronowitz, and others) who would use the tools furnished by postmodernism's critique of modernist education as a means to achieve emancipatory ends. But this is not necessarily the case. Postmodernism's delegitimization of modernism (and, by extension, of modernist education), may represent an opportunity for the function of teachers, students, and even the curriculum to be reimagined. In the third space between the metanarrative of the modernist curriculum and the lived narratives of the classroom, the possibility of hybridity and change exists.

Henry Giroux refers to this location as capable of sustaining a "border pedagogy" of resistance and change (1991). Fundamentally political in its means and anti-racist and emancipatory in its ends, border pedagogy is aimed at providing educators with "the opportunity to rethink the relations between the centers and the margins of power" (Giroux 1993a, 481). For Giroux, border pedagogy involves an investigation on the part of both teachers and students of how the "dominant culture works to exercise power [and] how to resist power which is oppressive" (p. 485). The notion that border pedagogy involves a careful reading of the values and beliefs embedded in modernist culture ties it closely to the deconstructionist emphasis of postmodernism. But knowledge of the "deep structural factors" (Hall 1981, 61) that influence society is not enough. Border pedagogy insists on a democratic redefinition of the curriculum that legitimates the identity and experiences of students in a manner that mirrors the concept of *currere* developed by William Pinar and Grumet (1976).

Structured around the idea that the curriculum is the ongoing process of running the race rather than the tangible object of the racecourse itself, *currere* implies that an understanding of the curriculum lies in each individual's experience of the curriculum. With this focus, the lived experience and identity of each participant in the race becomes critical to an understanding of the race itself. In effect, there are multiple narratives of the race (the curriculum), but these multiple narratives can be shared. As William Schubert notes in his discussion of Pinar and Grumet's concept:

> Based on the idea of sharing of autobiographical accounts with others who strive for similar understanding, the curriculum becomes a reconceiving of one's perspective on life. It also becomes a social process whereby individuals come to greater understanding of themselves, others, and the world through mutual reconceptualization. (1986, 33)

This same emphasis on the validity of individual experience and on "mutual reconception" emerges in Giroux's border pedagogy. Giroux notes that an emancipatory border pedagogy encourages students to "air their feelings from the perspective of the subject positions they experience as constitutive of their own identities" but cautions that these individual experiences should be highlighted as part of the "historical, cultural, and social practices that serve to either undermine or to reconstruct democratic public life" (1993a, 483–84).

It is through this emphasis on the legitimacy of individual experience and on the need to share these diverse experiences in order to create some broader meaning or understanding that border pedagogy intersects with hermeneutics. Combining the political, dialogic, and fundamentally emancipatory thrust of postmodern border pedagogy with the hermeneutic quest for meaning creates conditions under which action research can become a successful response to the ambiguity and difficulty of classroom teaching.

Part II: Hermeneutics

Pedagogically, the highest priority is in having children and young people
gain precisely a sense of the human world as being a narrative construction
that can be entered and enjoyed creatively; to have a sense that received
understanding can be interpreted and re-interpreted and that human
responsibility is fulfilled in precisely a taking up of this task. (Smith 1995,
23)

Because hermeneutics focuses on the interpretation of the meaning of
any text, it is an approach well suited to both postmodernism and
educational action research. Its focus on the uniqueness of individual
interpretation and on the problematic nature of universal understanding
makes the discipline open to the deconstructive aspect of postmodernism.
Paul Ricoeur (1981), for example, notes the fundamental anti-modernist
stance of hermeneutics when he notes that the discipline proceeds from
the premise that we do not understand. And, at least in its moderate form,
its emphasis on the need to carefully attend to the distinctiveness of
individual voices while at the same time attempting to jointly achieve
what Hans-Georg Gadamer termed a "fusion of horizons" of meaning
(1975, 101) mirrors the joint cycle of questioning, reflection, and action
that guides collaborative action research. Thus, hermeneutics, in Hilly
Bernard's terms, "confronts the issue of ambiguity, interpretation,
intentionality and meaning and asserts the inescapable subjective in
human inquiry" (1994, 10).

With its emphasis on subjectivity, interpretation, and ambiguity,
hermeneutics shares with postmodernism a resistance to definition
(Slattery 1995). And, as is the case with postmodernism's stance on
metanarratives, hermeneutics rejects the idea that the ultimate meaning
of any text can be established. As David Jardine notes, any attempt to
suggest that transcendent understanding can be achieved is more than
merely problematic; it is fundamentally an act of domination that seeks
to "render the world a harmless picture for our indifferent and
disinterested perusal" (1992, 118–19). This criticism of the Cartesian
desire for duality and control closely matches the postmodern critique of
the Enlightenment project. But hermeneutics represents more than
critique, more than problematization. For John Caputo it represents an
attempt to "restore life to its original difficulty" (1987, 1). And it is in
this attempt that a clear distinction emerges between postmodernism and
the hermeneutic tradition.

Restoration first involves an examination of the structures within which the operation must take place. The critique of modernism by hermeneutics is essentially a critique of the techno-scientific discourse that underlies modernism (Gadamer 1981). That discourse is predicated on the view that both the human and natural sciences present a series of "problems" that can be resolved by careful observation, reason, and logic (Jardine 1992). Implicit in this model is the primacy of reason and objectivity over intuition and subjectivity (Borgmann 1992). But the triumph of what Charles Taylor refers to as "instrumental reason" (Taylor 1991, 5) carries with it significant dangers. In the first place it delegitimizes individual experience except insofar as that experience mirrors a preexisting objective reality. In doing so, reason becomes "a series of unrelated assertions bereft of memory" (Saul 1992, 139). In the second place, decontextualized reason assumes the mantle of conceptual ideal, and in this guise it provides a justification for the most unreasonable actions. Referring to the consequences of this transformation, John Caputo writes: "Reason has had a fortune not unlike 'God' and 'country': some of the worst violence is committed in its name" (Caputo 1987, 210).

When applied to research, the techno-scientific approach becomes oriented toward closure and preoccupied with theorizing and problem-solving (Schon 1991; Beyer and Liston, 1996). But this teleological preoccupation is not necessarily appropriate to the study of human existence—Gadamer, for example, warns against the "naive surrender to the experts of social technology" (1976, 40). And, as Misgeld and Jardine point out, this orientation precludes the notions of ambiguity and difficulty that seem to characterize much of the lived experience of teachers and students. In fact, in its search for answers to the *problem* of education, the goal of techno-scientific appears to be silence, "the end of the need to address such issues" (Misgeld and Jardine, 1989, 236).

Hermeneutics seeks neither answers nor silence. Instead, it accepts the ambiguity that comes with interpretation. Thus, David Jardine emphasizes that hermeneutics is "concerned with the ambiguous nature of life itself" (Jardine, 1992, 119). But it is this very "ability to see what is questionable" (Gadamer, 1976, 13) that marks the hermeneutic search for meaning. Hermeneutics is not to be equated with the search for absolute meaning or even with the reinvention of some more human and humane metanarrative. Rather, it is a difficult and tentative exploration in which the role of interpretation, in David Smith's terms, is "to show what is at work in different disciplines and, in the service of human generativity and good faith, is [to be] engaged in the mediation of meaning" (Smith 1991, 187).

The theme of hermeneutics as the mediation of meaning implies the existence of both a purpose and a community. For Richard Rorty, that purpose is nothing less than to occupy a middle ground between "reliance on a God-surrogate and on one's individual preferences" (1997, 526). Such a middle ground is predicated on moving toward "realization of the potentialities that have already been sketched out in the language we are now using—toward realization of our present vaguely sense ideals" (ibid.). But the middle ground is ground held in common and thus for Rorty, hermeneutics leads to the recognition that reliance on the "common sense of community to which one belongs" (p. 527) is the best location for working out a shared human existence.

In its emphasis on the search for meaning through interpretation and on the critical importance of shared experience within the hermeneutic circle, hermeneutics appears to differ radically from postmodernism, yet some scholars have argued that the two are inextricably linked. Patrick Slattery, for example, asserts that "all discourses about postmodernism are interpretative and hermeneutic endeavors" (1995, 104). But in this approach Slattery substitutes means for ends. Hermeneutics certainly has a deconstructive aspect that suggests that meaning is necessarily contextual and contingent, but its ends are more fundamentally emancipatory. When Gadamer speaks of a "fusion of horizons of meaning" David Jardine describes hermeneutics as helping us live out our lives together, and Richard Rorty notes that hermeneutic interpretation leads to the discovery of a sense of community, they are all referring to the common hermeneutic attempt to achieve clarity faced with what Roberto Alejandro describes as "a backdrop of different and conflicting traditions" (1993, 36).

However hermeneutics does not present a uniform face to the researcher. As is the case with postmodernism, there are different currents within the discipline, and the application of hermeneutics to education itself carries with it a certain imperative that tends to emphasize its instrumental function. In terms of the "faces" of hermeneutics noted above, it is possible to discern three distinct orientations in hermeneutics. Shaun Gallagher (1992) has classified these orientations as conservative, moderate and radical hermeneutics. Following an examination of these three orientations, I suggest that a combination of moderate and radical hermeneutics is most suited to the research carried out for this book and, in a more general sense, to educational action research itself.

Conservative Hermeneutics

The conservative hermeneutic tradition is predicated on the view that meaning is relatively fixed and that it is embodied in language structures that are themselves discernible and universal. From this perspective, the meaning of any text can be clearly established; the aim of interpretation is to use the appropriate techniques to uncover that meaning (Gallagher 1992). Based on the nineteenth-century work of Friederich Schleiermacher and his successor Wilhelm Dilthey, conservative hermeneutics expanded the focus of interpretation beyond the attempt to understand biblical texts to the attempt to understand human experience (Slattery 1995). Thus, Dilthey wrote that hermeneutic interpretation was as critical to an understanding of the human sciences (*Geisteswissenschaften*) as empiricism was to an understanding of the natural sciences (*Naturwissenschaften*) (Dilthey in Howard 1982).

Dilthey and other conservative hermeneutic scholars such as Emilio Betti and E.D. Hirsch accepted the fact that both a text and its interpreter could be trapped in a particular historical context, but at the same time they asserted that with careful and diligent application of the right methodology, hermeneutic interpretation could reveal the objective meaning of any text (Gallagher 1992).

For Dilthey, the work of understanding a text meant recourse to what he termed a "hermeneutic circle" in which knowledge of the background or context of each passage was critical to understand those that came before and after it. At the same time, understanding the whole meant understanding each of its parts. This process was ongoing and had no beginning or endpoint (Palmer 1969).

The contribution of conservative hermeneutics was to note that meaning was embedded in language and that this embeddedness affected the interpreter as much as it did the text. But its emphasis on the existence of objective truth and on the ability of method to reveal this truth limited its application to what Patrick Slattery terms the "traditional [and dehumanizing] technical approach to hermeneutics" (1995, 113).

Moderate Hermeneutics

In some ways, moderate hermeneutics has much in common with the sentiment Wilhelm Dilthey expressed when he noted that "the connectedness of psychic life is given as an original and general foundation" (Dilthey in Howard 1982, 15–16). This realization that there was a subjective component to understanding but that this subjectivity could be merged into a broader meaning finds its parallel in Paul Ricoeur's (1981) statement that "if meaning is not a segment of self-understanding, I don't know what it is" (56). But in the moderate hermeneutic tradition, that understanding can never achieve the level of objectivity.

This key point separates conservative from moderate hermeneutics. According to Gadamer (1975), the interpretation of any text is always affected by the prejudices of the interpreter. But for Gadamer, they were the vehicles through which a text was opened to understanding. These prejudices, which he termed "blind prejudices" and "justified prejudices," both condition and bias the interpreter. For this reason they needed to be "raise[d] to awareness" before meaningful interpretation could take place, and those prejudices that were blind or unproductive needed to be jettisoned (Gadamer 1975, 291). Although criticized by Emilio Betti for his "loss of objectivity" (Betti in Gallagher 1992, 14), Gadamer did not suggest that meaning was irrevocably subjective.

Instead he emphasized the act of interpretation as an act of creativity in which both the reader and the author participate in the creation of meaning (Gallagher 1992, 10). This dialogic conversation between the interpreter and the text returns hermeneutics back to Dilthey's hermeneutic circle, but for Gadamer the hermeneutic circle was more than a method of interpretation; it implied a relationship between the participants. Thus:

> Each [person] is at first a kind of linguistic circle, and these linguistic circles come in contact with each other, merging more and more. Language occurs once again, in vocabulary and grammar as always, and never without the inner infinity of the dialogue that is in process between every speaker and his [or her] partner. That is the fundamental dimension of hermeneutics. (1976, 17)

For David Blacker, this act of creation or "fusion of horizons" that takes place in the hermeneutic circle marks the humanism of Gadamer's hermeneutics which contrasts with the bias toward structuralism of conservative hermeneutics. As Blacker notes:

> sharing in this historically constituted conversation does not mean that I experience tradition as the opinion of some person or other, but than I am able to enter into a game made up of myself and other persons but not reducible to any one of us. (1993, 7)

The prejudices and biases that underlie and constrain the dialogic nature of the hermeneutic conversation between the interpreter and the text make the establishment of the ultimate meaning of the text problematic. But the shared act of interpretation and reinterpretation that is characteristic of the hermeneutic circle allows for meaning to emerge from the conversation.

Yet underlying this assumption is an ethical concern. In effect, the implication is that there are "rules" to the game that David Blacker refers to. If shared meaning is to emerge from hermeneutic discourse, then the participants in this discourse must be willing to engage in what Gadamer refers to "genuine conversation" (Gadamer 1975) in which both parties "have the good will to try to understand one another" (Gadamer in Gallagher 1992, 23).

In its aim of shared interpretation and in the "ethic of collaboration" that moderate hermeneutics implies, a wide range of possibilities is opened up for education and for educational research. Furthermore, conceived of as both an ethic and an approach to collaboration, moderate hermeneutics has much in common with the technique and the aims of action research.

Radical Hermeneutics

Radical hermeneutics shares, along with postmodernism, a deep suspicion of the idea that language can be a kind of transcendent device for fixing meaning. In fact, for its proponents (David Jardine, John Caputo, Gary Madison), the purpose of radical hermeneutic interpretation is not to establish meaning at all, but rather to establish the principle of contingency (Gallagher 1992). But in the notion that all interpretative acts are relative and contingent, radical hermeneutics rejects the possibility of the fusion of horizons that Gadamer sets forth as the aim of hermeneutics. For Shaun Gallagher, such an approach comes perilously close to nihilism (p. 10).

However, closer examination of the writings of radical hermeneutic scholars brings to light both the moral base that lies at the root of radical hermeneutics and the *engagement* with the world such a moral stance implies. A closer reading of radical hermeneutics suggests how aspects of this orientation can be added to moderate hermeneutics to better fit the relatively inflexible dictates of the school environment.

Gary Madison, for example, suggests that a hermeneutic understanding of experience is a transformative act in which the individual changes both himself and the world with which he has contact (1988, 189). The notion that radical hermeneutics implies involvement can also be seen in the writings of John Caputo. In Caputo's terms, the ambiguity that emerges out of the radical hermeneutic perspective that meaning is both contingent and relative implies action rather than stasis, opportunity rather than indifference. Writing of this opportunity he notes: "It is precisely the uncertainty of things, which links us indissolubly, which commits us to the dispersal of power structures, which think they have the final word" (1987, 288).

But in what amounts to a call for a pedagogy of resistance, a moral imperative can be heard; there is in Caputo's writing a sense that there are better worlds. This same imperative emerges in David Jardine's work. Noting, along with Caputo, that ambiguity represents both a dilemma and a space in which we can learn to live with the "vibrant difficulty" that characterizes our lives, Jardine concludes, "It is unimaginable to bring new life into a world in which there is nothing left to say. How can we want this and be educators as well?" (1992, 126). Thus for Caputo and Jardine, radical hermeneutics, in pointing out the impossibility of having the "last Word," challenges modernist concepts of perfectibility and closure.

But in doing so, it also challenges hermeneutic orientations that suggest that meaning—even in the more contingent Gadamerist sense—can be transcendent. However, in the work of Jardine and Caputo, in particular, the marriage of the twin notions of ambiguity and difficulty to a moral stance that implies action contributes a critical edge to the more moderate hermeneutics of Gadamer and Ricoeur. And in the spirit of eclecticism that postmodernism implies, the fusion of aspects of moderate and radical hermeneutics holds great promise for linking educational research and practice.

Hermeneutics and Education

In its emphasis on interpretation and on understanding, hermeneutics has much to contribute to education. Shaun Gallagher notes these possibilities when he writes:

> If education involves understanding and interpretation; if formal educational practice is guided by the use of texts and commentary, reading and writing; ...if educational experience is a temporal process involving fixed expressions of life and the transmission or critique of traditions; if, in effect, education is a human enterprise, then hermeneutics, which claims all of these as its subject matter, holds out the promise of providing a deeper understanding of the educational process. (1992, 24)

Patrick Slattery discusses the possibilities of hermeneutics in similarly optimistic terms. Hermeneutic discourse, he concludes involves a "community circle of creative interpretation that respects the interplay of individuals and groups to which they belong and which [incorporates this interplay] into the fabric of schooling" (1991, 119). But is this optimism justified? Are the acts of creativity and the deeper understanding that Slattery and Gallagher refer to possible within the context of modern education? David G. Smith who has written eloquently about the potential of hermeneutics is much less sanguine. Attempts to engage in hermeneutic inquiry, he warns, are dangerous: "Students of hermeneutics should be mindful that their interpretations could lead them into trouble with the 'authorities'" (1991, 187).

A wealth of scholarship (Foucault 1980; Giroux 1983; Apple 1998; Giddens 1990; Flax 1990; Lather 1991) has noted the traditions of power and authority that lie embedded in the curriculum and in language itself. While any attempt to reveal and to call into questions these traditions may carry with it a certain moral imperative, it is nevertheless a difficult undertaking. This is particularly so for classroom teachers. Their position on the margins of the chain of authority that determines curriculum content and the "intensification" of those duties—standardized evaluation and adherence to "district" educational philosophies, for example—mark a progressive and debilitating loss of independence (Apple 1998). Faced with this loss of autonomy, it seems just as likely that teachers will face inward toward the security that comes from turning toward their "minimal selves" (Lasch 1984) rather than looking outward in anticipation of the emancipatory possibilities of hermeneutic discourse.

Yet in the face of these very real dangers of disempowerment and disengagement, hermeneutics represents an opportunity to ask questions about how meaning is derived in education and how we as teachers are situated in that derivation. In that sense, it has exciting implications for both curriculum and for "professional development" in the truest sense of the word.

A hermeneutically inspired curriculum is one in which there is opportunity to bring to light what is questionable (Gadamer 1976). Through the hermeneutic investigation of those prejudices that situate us in a particular historical tradition, there is opportunity to see both how we are guided and constrained by our prejudices and how those prejudices influence our relations with others. With this realization comes the possibility that teachers and students can form their own hermeneutic circle in which the Cartesian assumptions that imply that the world is a known or, in principle, knowable object and that the teacher is a source of knowledge and the student an empty vessel, is bypassed in favor of a more ambiguous and democratic relationship in which students and teachers can ask questions together.

But the focus of a hermeneutic curriculum is not to replace one method of classroom instruction with another. For hermeneutics to contribute to education, it must be viewed as more than "one more damn thing" (Smith in Jardine 1992, 124) that holds the false promise of answers to the question of education. Richard Rorty discusses this issue in some depth in his essay "Hermeneutics, General Studies and Teaching." Using the example of a hermeneutic approach to the study of history and the humanities, he notes:

> Hermeneutics contributes the perspective that history and the humanities [are not] monuments of unaging intellect but a series of attempts—sometimes-heroic attempts—to cope with problems which were not ours, but were similar enough to offer us useful hints. We will not get instructions about what to do, but rather models of the sort of virtue that we must exemplify. (1997, 530)

Viewed from a hermeneutic perspective, history and, by extension, national identity are simultaneously "de-canonized" and localized. As Roberto Alejandro reminds us, from a hermeneutic perspective "every generation cannot forfeit the responsibility of reflecting on its own circumstances" (1993, 113). In this reflective process, students and teachers do not stand outside of history, they reside within it.   Their personal struggles are, in a sense, historicized by making them part of the ongoing (and historical) process of making meaning of their lives.

Characteristics of a Hermeneutic Approach to Education

The question of how, in more practical terms, a hermeneutic approach to education would look is addressed in several scholarly sources.   Two key characteristics appear to typify both the hermeneutic curriculum and the hermeneutic classroom. The first presents teachers with new pedagogies; the second suggests significant alterations to what should be considered the "curriculum" itself.

Approached from David Jardine's perspective that the function of hermeneutics is not to dispel the tension that comes from a life lived in ambiguity, "but to live and speak from within it" (1992, 126), the hermeneutic curriculum can be conceived as a series of ongoing hermeneutic circles the purpose of which is to explore the difficulty of life.

But this exploration can only be achieved if the participants in the circle are free to speak. This implies a way of acting that "opens up" the classroom yet remains focused on achieving common understandings. For Peter Taubman, this delicate balance represents a "midpoint" between teachers' conferred identity as "teachers" and the desire to shed this identity and interact with students as equals. Taubman refers to this midpoint as situated between the "one who knows and the one who cares" (1992, 233).

This space, itself an ambiguous location, confirms Caputo and Jardine's notions of "difficulty," but it implies more than a desirable (if problematic) site for the introduction of a hermeneutic curriculum.   It also implies a place where a Gadamerian "fusion of horizons" can be achieved.   Such a fusion can take place only if the traditions and experiences of all the participants in the hermeneutic circle can be brought forth.   This kind of "situated facilitation" is the role of the teacher in hermeneutic inquiry.

The second characteristic of a hermeneutic approach to education links the hermeneutic circle to the curriculum. It is bound to the valorization of the experiences of students and teachers that the hermeneutic circle suggests. For Joe Kinchloe and William Pinar (1991), this valorization implies extensive use of autobiography in the classroom. As Pinar notes: "Our life histories are not liabilities to be exorcised but are the very precondition to knowing" (1988, 150). But in a hermeneutic sense, these life histories form the "text" (the curriculum) for interpretation. Susan Edgerton, for example, emphasizes that the worth in the relation of student experiences lies in gaining "more complex and subtle" understandings of self and other (1991, 97). In *Teaching against the Grain,* Roger Simon makes the same point while warning that student experiences cannot be made part of schooling without rigorous examination of these experiences. Teachers, he writes, must recognize "the centrality of the pedagogical problem of both legitimizing student experiences as appropriate curriculum content [while] at the same time working to challenge such experiences" (1992, 135).

For Madeleine Grumet, whose 1976 collaboration with William Pinar produced *Toward a Poor Curriculum* (Pinar and Grumet 1976), a seminal work on the role of autobiography in the curriculum, autobiography can itself be a kind of middle ground, mediating between self and other.   Thus, while autobiography does not "effect the total reconciliation between subjectivity and objectivity" it can, nevertheless, "commit us to acknowledge the paradox" (Grumet 1988, 42).

In its emphasis on the multiplicity of voices that form the educational hermeneutic circle and in the idea that the curriculum can and should incorporate these voices, hermeneutics has much in common with action research. Discussing his approach to action research, Terry Carson refers to the discipline as a "hermeneutics of practice" that focuses on the concept of "interpretative knowing" (1992, 112–14). These links will be explored later, but given that action research forms the most critical research orientation of this study, an exploration of the origin, evolution, and current status of the discipline is a necessary precursor to discussing the research project itself.

Part III: Action Research

In action research, the intention to affect social practice stands shoulder to shoulder with the intention to understand it. (Kemmis in Smits 1994, 33)

The roots of action research are firmly embedded in social democratic tradition that views activism as a way of implementing progressive changes in society (Lewin 1988). This moral orientation toward "the good" is described more concretely by Abraham Shumsky as "activating the social and spiritual life of the community in a continuous search for self-improvement" (Shumsky 1988, 81). But in order to achieve what are fundamentally democratic and emancipatory ends, traditional approaches to the idea of research itself had to be rejected. Based on Kurt Lewin's conviction that: "Research that produces nothing but books will not suffice" (Lewin 1990, 41), action research has consciously attempted to bridge the gap between theory and practice that exists in other research orientations.

In distinguishing the three main constituents of educational action research, Wolfgang Klafki highlights how action research proposes that this gap between practice and theory is to be closed. Thus educational action research takes as its starting point educational practice itself. Second, it takes place in cooperation with the educational practice it aims to change. In this regard Klafki writes: "It is thus not the case that research is developed outside the practice. The research is developed in cooperation with people working on educational problems in practice" (1988, 253). And finally, it abolishes the Cartesian character of most research. That is, it removes the division between researchers and subjects.

Philosophically, then, action research attempts to "reject the fiction that we can detach ourselves and become merely objective observers" (Carson 1992, 111). From a functional perspective this implies a research process that is both collaborative and democratic. In Nevitt Sandford's terms, this process engages all its participants in a continuous cycle of "analysis, fact-finding, conceptualization, planning, execution, more fact-finding or evaluation; and then a repetition of this whole circle of activities; indeed a spiral of such circles" (1988, 127).

What distinguishes action research from many other research orientations is the critical notion that change can emerge as much *through* the research process as it can as a *result* of the findings of the research (Elliott 1991, 50). The emphasis on the process of research being (at least) as critical as its endpoint makes action research share some of the same terrain as hermeneutics. In fact Sanford's definition of the endless spiral of action research has much in common with Dilthey's hermeneutic circle.

But in a very important sense, action research is not, like hermeneutics, consciously searching to mediate between competing and possibly irreconcilable subjectivities. The location of action research is necessarily the midpoint itself or rather, a series of midpoints: between theory and practice, between the curriculum as plan and the curriculum as lived experience, between the teacher as source of knowledge and the teacher as learner. It has no rational for existence, nor can it survive except in the spaces in between. And this is the very location in which teachers must construct their professional lives. For this reason, action research is uniquely suited to educational research. This seems particularly true when one recalls Wolfgang Klafki's (1988) assertion that educational research must take educational practice as both its starting position and endpoint.

However, if action research is to be genuinely transformative in both its ends and its means, some technique for allowing the participants to examine the research process in a critical way is essential. The most commonly accepted approach to provide for this examination is reflection, (Carr and Kemmis 1983; Elliott 1991; Carson 1992)

Reflection links both the life experiences of those involved in action research with the research issues they are engaged in investigating. In Carr and Kemmis's terms, "[Action research] involves discovering correspondences and non-correspondences between understandings and practices (for example by counterposing such categories as rhetoric and reality or theory and practice)" (1983, 182).

But reflection needs to carry with it some other dimension to be capable of moving beyond mere subjective interpretation to more generalizable understandings. For many action researchers, this other dimension is critical theory. From a critical theory stance, action research relies on a conception of knowledge that implies that truth and action are both "socially-constructed and historically embedded" (pp. 182–83). From this perspective, the participants in action research are engaged in a process that can lead to both personal and general emancipation (Elliott 1991). And the process of identity formation itself becomes a key aspect of the research process. As Madeleine Grumet notes, education itself becomes a metaphor for a "dialogue with the world of his or her own experience" (1988, 29).

But comparing Carr and Kemmis's observations with those of Grumet reveals a significant gap between the more socially reconstructive action research of Lewin and those, such as Carr, Kemmis, and McTaggert, who have been labeled as representative of the Deakin School of action research, on the one hand, and the more reflective approach to individual understanding typified by Terrance Carson, William Pinar, Ted Aoki, and Clermont Gauthier, on the other.

While these differences serve to point out the evolving nature of the discipline, they also point to critically different philosophical orientations that have significant repercussions for the nature and intent of educational action research.

Action Research as Critical Theory

For Carr, Kemmis, McTaggart, and others, whose work in action research emerged out of Deakin University, action research is primarily emancipatory in its aim. Carr and Kemmis, in particular, view action research as a form of "critical educational science" (1983, 117) whose aim is to effect cultural change more than it is to initiate improvements in individual practice. For example, Kemmis and McTaggart note that: "improving education is not just a matter of *individual action*, it is also a matter of *cultural action*. It means changing both at the individual level and at the level of the culture of the group of which the individual is a member" (1988, 34).

This stress on cultural change places the Deakin School firmly within the framework of critical theory—particularly the work of Jürgen Habermas. Habermas's emphasis on the need to create a critical social science in opposition to the deformations imposed on the individual by objectivist social science (Bleicher 1980, 154) implies both a methodology and an end that stresses emancipation. This same emancipatory process and end can be seen in the Deakin School. Grundy and Kemmis in their overview of action research in Australia note, for example, that action research is "inherently social" in its orientation and that, for this reason, "action researchers are inevitably concerned with the politics and processes of innovation and change" (1988, 321). And later, quoting Habermas, they conclude, "As Habermas says: 'in a process of enlightenment, there can be only participants'" (p. 334).

But this emphasis on critical reflection as a technique in emancipatory educational action research has been criticized by those who see in such an approach a return to metanarratives of control in what amounts to a reification of modernism. John Elliott, for example, condemns the critical orientation of the Deakin School for what he sees as a return to the domination of theoretical constructs over the validity of individual experience, noting that such an approach appears to "deny the possibility that teachers' self-understandings of their practices can alone constitute a source of critical self-reflection and emancipatory action" (1991, 116).

And Paul Smith notes ironically that research that bases itself on critical theory alone seems unable to ask the question of

> why some people—those living their relation to their condition of existence through the categories of a distorted ideology—cannot recognize that it is distorted, while we, [researchers] with our superior wisdom, or armed with properly formed concepts, can. (1988, 11)

The externally focused, social-reconstructionist orientation of critical action research stands in sharp contrast to the emphasis on action research as an exploration how to live and act within "ambiguities, conflicts and tensions" that mark the classroom experience of teachers (Elliott 1991, 116).   Such an emphasis characterizes the work of Terrance Carson, Clermont Gauthier, John Elliott, and Ted Aoki.

Action Research as Reflective and Lived Practice

Ted Aoki was among the first scholars to attempt to delineate the parameters of the ambiguous location teachers occupy. The important observation he makes regarding the tension that exists between the "curriculum as plan" and the "curriculum as lived experience" (T. Aoki 1988) marks a critical point of departure for the investigation of classroom practice.   Implied in his observation is the unique "situatedness" of the experience of classroom teaching, but a more crucial implication is that any investigation of classroom practice must begin with the self-perceptions of teachers.   Thus, the issue of what teaching is cannot be separated from the question of what it is to be a teacher. For Aoki then, it is critical that research about teaching calls us to "in-dwell in the earthy place where we experience daily life with our colleagues and students, and begin our search for the 'isness' of teaching, for the being of teaching" (1992, 20).

This search for the "isness" of teaching is not bound up with essentializing descriptions, nor should it be linked to attempts to resolve the "problem" of education. Rather, it returns the field of action research to the difficulty and ambiguity of the daily life of the classroom. But unlike critically oriented action research, it is neither ideologically bound nor externally oriented. In Clermont Gauthier's (1992) terms, reflective action research is oriented around the practical question of what to do.

This same emphasis on "in-dwelling," reflection, and "situated action" emerges in Terry Carson's research. Describing his research orientation as "interpretative knowing" Carson, reflecting Aoki's concerns, emphasizes the need to "reground our [theoretical] understandings in practice" (1992, 113). But his approach does not represent a reification of theory in a slightly more pragmatic guise. Instead, Carson stresses the need to conceive of teaching as a "living practice" in which teachers and students "see themselves as inextricably tied to the complex relations that form various layers of communities" (1997, xvii).

Conclusion

In its acceptance of contingency and ambiguity and its stress on the critical importance of individual interpretation, reflective action research carries with it elements of postmodernism and hermeneutics. The approaches and aims of these three research orientations make them particularly suited to educational research that takes the lived experience of the classroom as its starting point. In Chapter 3, I discuss how classrooms have increasingly become absurd spaces and how action research (in particular) represents a way to live with/in absurdity.

CHAPTER 3
Five Teachers in Search of a Narrative

> What we're doing here is trying to see where what we think fits into what the "experts" tell us. I know all five of us have strong views on what we think of nationalism. But it's strange to think of us arguing with them about it.
>
> —Peter

Introduction: Into the Realm of the Ambiguous and the Absurd

In his 1985 work *Prophets of Extremity,* Allan Megill discusses the experience of poststructuralism in terms of the "latent absurdity" that comes of residing within a "state of tension with the given" (1985, 365). In certain respects, this book is an examination of the latent absurdity that resides in the curriculum and within teachers who, not infrequently, find themselves situated in the same state of tension that Megill so aptly describes. In particular, however, this book examines the Canadian national identity: how it is portrayed in the curricula, how classroom teachers perceive it, and how it is essential that the concept be both reconsidered and reimagined if it is to retain any significance for our students.[1]

As I noted in Chapter 1, the genesis of this book lay in an action research project focusing on classroom teachers' changing perceptions of nationalism in the post-Cold War era. In the course of the discussions that emerged around the topic, it became clear that the teachers' conceptions of nationalism were bound closely to their own, very personal, understandings of national identity and that there was a growing uneasiness with the way national identity and particularly Canadian identity was described in the curriculum. This unease that Megill has named the "state of tension with the given" ultimately became the problem position that determined the location of my research. In this sense, it is critical to examine the first project that generated both the topic of this book (teacher perceptions of national identity) and the research methodologies (action research informed by hermeneutics and postmodernism) that I chose to apply.

In any examination of contemporary education, the notion of absurdity has particular resonance for classroom teachers and action researchers alike.[2] Most teaching professionals have experienced the tension between the curriculum as plan and the curriculum as lived experience (T. Aoki 1988). One teacher described this tension as emerging from the ironic knowledge that "beneath what appeared as a smooth surface much uncertainty and discontinuity existed" (Connelly and Clandinin 1999, 14). Jardine discusses this experience in terms of the paralyzing and ultimately exhausting Enlightenment-driven desire to use education to achieve "mastery" over knowledge (124).

In the light of the ambiguous location that most classroom teachers speak from and the environment that much of action research plays itself out in, absurdism has much to say to those who advocate action research in the field of curriculum development. In its rejection of modernist intellectual structures, of the philosophy of reductionism, and of the idea of shared meaning itself, absurdism celebrates the subjective, perhaps unknowable, experience of each individual (Esslin 1987, 23). These aspects of absurdism are clearly reflected in action research. For example, in his discussion of action research, Clermont Gauthier renounces all those structures (location, time frame, theory, and phenomenological methodology) that typically characterize modernist research and separate the "researcher" from his or her "subjects." Gauthier further refuses to "essentialize" (and by extension limit) the discipline through any attempt to define it, focusing instead on "how it works, and what it does" (1992, 185). This emphasis on the process and practicality of action research is echoed in the work of Terry Carson who notes that a key premise of action research is that "we may simultaneously inform and change ourselves" (1992, 102).

Broad intellectual similarities aside, there are parallels between absurdism and action research that present the researcher with ambiguous situations and uncomfortable realities. In my own action research group, which was composed of five classroom social studies teachers, there were more than a few "Beckettian" moments when we all waited for Godot. In particular, John, a veteran teacher whose attitude toward the action research project reflected his practical approach to teaching, served as a constant if not always welcome link between the group and absurdism. Despite his enthusiasm for our discussions of the meaning of nationalism in the post-Cold War era, near the end of most sessions he would quickly bring us back to ground with the unanswerable but nevertheless critical question: "OK, so where do we go from here?" At such times I found some comfort in dialogue from

Samuel Beckett's play *Endgame,* in which two characters capture both
the essence of absurdism and one of the essential dilemmas of action
research:

> Ham: We're not beginning to...to...mean something?
> Clov: Mean something? You and I *mean* something? (Beckett, 1958, 32–33)

The absurdist genre's investigation of whether "others" can, in fact,
"mean" something is central to action research, and it also became the
location for much of my own action research project. Our discussions
were hermeneutic in nature and frequently reflected the attempts of
hermeneutics to "confront the issues of complexity, ambiguity,
interpretation, intentionality and meaning" in a manner that "asserts the
inescapable subjective in human inquiry" (Bernard in Slattery 1995,
105). But if we often failed to achieve Hans-Georg Gadamer's "fusion
of horizons" of meaning (1975, 101) the exercise itself was empowering.
We were, in effect, "others" discussing "others." Teachers, themselves
traditionally "de-authorized," (Foucault, 1972; Boii 1993) and held
outside the dominant discourse realm in educational research, reflecting
on the post-Cold War meaning of the rise of ethnic nationalism and
changing our classroom practices in response to those collaborative
reflections.

Prologue: Nationalism as the Setting

The focus of this initial action research project was the problem of the
reemergence of nationalism in the post-Cold War era. Was it essentially
a constructive force with ties to nineteenth-century nation building and
twentieth-century decolonization, as it had usually been portrayed in the
curriculum, or did it carry with it unlooked-for connotations that required
classroom teachers to rethink their definition of the term? Scholarly
opinion on the implications of resurgent nationalism was clearly divided.
Those on the political left such as Renata Salecl (1994) and Julia
Kristeva (1993) tended to see emergent European nationalism in terms of
a dangerous retrograde step, one that reintroduced national chauvinism
and racism to the political scene. On the political right, commentators
such as Francis Fukuyama (1992) tended to downplay its importance and
focus instead on the positive benefits of the post-Cold War triumph of
western-style democracy and market-driven economies. Others like
Michael Ignatieff (1993) and Benjamin Barber (1995) emphasized that

the clash between ethnically based nationalism and more broadly based forms of nationalism was a product of the post-Cold War era that deserved more careful examination.

In the face of these differing interpretations and given their own understandings of the post-Cold War rise of nationalism, my colleagues had key questions to ask about nationalism. How should we approach the topic? Was the social studies curriculum flexible enough to accommodate the changing nature of nationalism and the global community? How should we teach nationalism in our classrooms? Although these questions served as the focus for the dialogues that developed within our group, they were inevitably bound up in very subjective interpretations of nationalism, national identity, and personal identity, and they continually revealed the link between teaching and the realm of the absurd.

The dialogues themselves revolved around three texts that I presented to the group for analysis and reflection. Each text was chosen for the different stance of the author on post-Cold War nationalism. The first was the much-discussed and highly controversial study *The End of History* written by Francis Fukuyama (1992), then deputy director of the U.S. State Department. The second was an excerpt from Michael Ignatieff's (1993) examination of nationalism, *Blood and Belonging*. And the third was the introduction to Julia Kristeva's *Nations Without Nationalism* (1993). These three texts with radically diverging views on the nature of nationalism were the individual "acts" in the absurdist drama that subsequently played itself out.

Act I. Becoming Absurd: The Death of Certainty

> Look, I know that a lot of things are changing in the world, but I don't always have the time to deal with them in the classroom. And if I tried to deal with it all I wouldn't be able to get my students ready for the Diploma Exam, and if these kids do badly, I know I'll catch shit. (John, 1996)

The recent experience of teaching social studies at the senior high level has created its own pedagogy. Central to this new curriculum are the values of time management, production quotas (in the form of acceptable marks on standardized examinations), conformity, and caution. Although this is an implied criticism of the aims of neoliberal education, it is also an inescapable statement of fact. The "intense" (after Michael Apple 1993; 1998) reality of teaching in an environment that increasingly celebrates the passing on and evaluation of "received" wisdom. But these market-driven values increasingly fly in the face of the stated intent of most social studies curricula to promote the idea of "responsible citizenship;" these curricula typically define the concept in terms of the "critical thinking" that is basic to individuals who are "knowledgeable, purposeful [and who make] responsible choices" (Government of Alberta 1990, 3).

In itself, then, social studies curricula present teachers with an inherently absurdist dilemma as they find themselves trapped between the restrictive conditions imposed on them by society, a society of which they are inevitably a part, and their own, frequently contradictory, aspirations. It is, in effect, a double dilemma. The tension between the philosophical intents of social studies curricula that remain tentatively rooted in the social reconstructionist tradition of participatory democracy and its results-oriented demands that very much reflect current neoliberal economic theory is not easily reconciled. Although nationalism may have been the focus of the project, its location was and remained the realm of the absurd.

We began with a reading of an excerpt from Francis Fukuyama's book. Its central thesis was that the global triumph of economic liberalism not only ended the Cold War, it had also effectively "killed" history. Henceforth, peace and prosperity would characterize the new ahistorical age (Fukuyama 1992). The excerpt served as a useful introduction to nationalism because Fukuyama had labeled aggressive nationalism as the prime source in the "old," historical world, but Fukuyama's writing served another purpose: It brought the group together. We all rejected the premise that nationalism was a spent force. Given events subsequent to its publication (the rise of ethnic conflict in the former Soviet Union, the disintegration of Yugoslavia, and the dispute between ethnic Hutus and Tutsis in Rwanda), it was easy to dismiss Fukuyama's contentions. If anything, we agreed that nationalism was emerging as a much more powerful force than it had been at any time since the end of the Second World War. We were in accord; the article was incorrect. Jim was even more blunt in his assessment: "I mean this guy's a Ph.D.; how can he write such junk? My kids would pick this out as garbage in two seconds."

In the common criticism the group leveled at Fukuyama, a "voice" began to emerge. The possibility that the ideas of those usually defined as "experts" could be examined critically and even dismissed was a bit of a revelation, but for some of the teachers in the group it also presented a preliminary crisis of identity. Classroom teachers have traditionally been assigned a technical role in education as dispensers of expert knowledge (Giddens 1990). But if Fukuyama had gotten it so badly wrong, were there equally flawed interpretations of contemporary nationalism in the field? If we could, as a group, pick out the flaws in the "expert" publications on the subject, could we move beyond criticism to formulation? Could we develop our own interpretations of recent events in Bosnia or in the former Soviet Union, for example? Did we understand nationalism well enough to attempt this? As classroom teachers, did we even have the right to attempt such a task?

These questions necessarily involved blurring the lines between teaching and research, but they also held implications for our conceptions of our own identities as teachers. In more formal terms, the questions we had posed were both hermeneutic and absurdist. If we rejected the objective "truth" of Fukuyama's theories, and this was relatively easy for all of us to do, then we were faced with the necessity of either adopting another "expert" interpretation of nationalism or of formulating our own. In a sense, our dialogue with Fukuyama's idea had made us active participants in the on-going debate over what nationalism in the post-Cold War world means. But, once engaged in this debate, we were then obliged to act in a responsible manner if meaning was to be established. In this context, responsibility implied a willingness to examine our own ideas as well as those of others, to be prepared, in Gadamer's) words, to "raise to awareness those prejudices that guide and condition the process of understanding" (Gadamer in Gallagher 1992, 12).

Acknowledgment that both readers and authors bring their own biases to a text implies that a dialogic relationship exists between reader, text, and author. And in this relationship the possibility of creating shared perceptions exists. But although such an endeavor is clearly hermeneutic, it is equally clearly not absurdist. It is only in its more radical form, when hermeneutics discards the possibility of shared understanding and suggests instead that meaning is too subjective to be communicated (Caputo 1987), that absurdism and hermeneutics can be said to share the same zeitgeist.

The teachers involved in the group would never have considered themselves to be operating according to the dictates of radical hermeneutics, nor would they have seen themselves as players in some absurdist drama, but it seems clear that in the attempt to interpret Fukuyama's article and to confront our own understanding of nationalism, we were engaging in a fundamentally absurdist and hermeneutic process. In beginning to question the authoritative voices that traditionally informed and circumscribed their worldview, a world that Albert Camus had called the "familiar world of illusions and light" (1975, 13), the group had effectively "decentered" itself and opened itself up to a whole range of possible interpretations of nationalism in the post-Cold War world. This loss of certainty was not always comfortable, and it did not always lead us in predictable directions. But the essence of absurdism is coming to grips with the idea of absurdity itself. And the act of textual interpretation, even in moderate hermeneutics, also means abandoning the comfortable notion that transparent meaning can ever be attained.

As disquieting as the process of "becoming absurd" was for group members, and despite the fact that we were not always at ease in our discussions, we found ourselves confronting, at least indirectly, the critical hermeneutic and absurdist issues that inevitably emerged. When Fred commented that he found it much easier to teach as if the Cold War still existed rather than to try to make sense of all the complex and contradictory developments that had taken place since the breakup of the Soviet Union, he was coming to grips with the uncertainty of the absurd. And he was also expressing, by default, the view that John Caputo put forth that radical hermeneutics was "for the hardy and a discipline that [was] suspicious of the easy way out" (1987, 3).

Act II. Establishing an Absurdist Identity

> The point is who are you? Not why or how, not even what. You are the sum of so many reflections. How many reflections? Whose reflections? Is that what you consist of? (Pinter, 1961, iii)

The problem of establishing an authentic identity is not only an issue for absurdist drama; it is also inextricably linked to nationalism. But the question, for individuals as well as for nations, is: What is identity? It is a question that Canadians are painfully familiar with, and it became the core of the dialogues in the next stage of our action research project. We focused on Michael Ignatieff's examination of nationalism, *Blood and Belonging* (1993). Ignatieff's identification of ethnic nationalism as an essentially malign force set to usher in "a new age of violence" (p. 2) in the twenty-first century served as an effective counterpoint to Fukuyama's work, and it provided us with a touchstone for coming to grips with the relationship of nationalism to national identity.

In his book, Ignatieff presents two competing versions of nationalism. The first, civic nationalism, Ignatieff defines as an inclusive ideology linking all peoples—irrespective of race, gender, language, or ethnicity—to the political state. The second, ethnic nationalism, restricts nationality to those who share the same racial heritage (pp. 4–5). By this definition, ethnic nationalism is exclusive and racist, prone to xenophobia and always on the verge of violence toward those that are somehow "different" from the ruling ethnic group. Ignatieff writes with some concern that it is this second form of nationalism that has emerged as the dominant force on the world scene today (p. 2).

In our group, Ignatieff's depiction of ethnic nationalism as a violent, irrational force caused many debates, and it began to reveal differences in both our perceptions of nationalism and of our own identities. Some, like John, felt that ethnicity was essentially a positive force. For him, being Ukrainian meant having a strong sense of community and a strong sense of belonging. Civic nationalism, he felt, could be appreciated as a principle attaching the nation's citizens to the idea of the nation, but it remained devoid of any emotive component. As he commented after one particularly lively discussion, "Who can love a theory? It's what you are that counts." Others accepted Ignatieff's position. Allen pointed out the ethnic and sectarian violence that has continued to plague Northern Ireland and the Middle East. In his view, ethnicity was always divisive, and the only hope for peace, particularly in pluralistic nations, was the creation of some kind of unifying force that moved people beyond narrow identifications with limited communities.

The group's dialogues about Ignatieff's characterization of ethnic nationalism reemphasized the link between action research and absurdism in that we were engaged in a collaborative attempt to make meaning out of a particular question: in this case, how we interpreted post-Cold War nationalism. The collaboration we attempted revealed personal interpretations of the phenomenon that put us at odds with existing interpretations (the tension with the "given" that Megill notes), but our dialogues also revealed a growing division within the group about the nature of nationalism itself.

Frankly, when I initially called the group together, I was uncertain about whether it would work. The idea that teachers would be willing to give up what little free time they had to discuss an abstraction that might not have immediate or practical application to classroom teaching seemed more than somewhat optimistic. To my great surprise and infinite relief, however, my colleagues accepted the invitation with enthusiasm. More than that, it quickly became apparent through our discussions that most of them had thought about nationalism in some detail. Because action research involves the willingness to fully engage oneself in an uncertain and even uneasy dialogue with others, a dialogue that involves a certain amount of intellectual and emotional risk-taking, the commitment that Fred, John, Jim, and Allen made was impressive. And it carried with it an unspoken appreciation for the ironies of absurdism.

Like Vladimir and Estragon in *Waiting for Godot,* it was more than unlikely that we would reach any definitive answers about nationalism. Furthermore, it was unclear how the whole project itself could be brought to an end. Even our dialogues had a tone that came uncomfortably close to this passage from the play:

> Vladimir: Charming evening we're having
> Estragon: Unforgettable.
> Vladimir: And it's not over.
> Estragon: Apparently not.
> Vladimir: It's only the beginning.
> Estragon: It's awful. (Beckett 1959a, 34)

Thus Allen and Jim, in the process of sharing their perceptions of the progress of the project, engaged in the following exchange:

> Allen: I think we're finally getting someplace.
> Jim: I think you're right. I think I've got a better perspective on nationalism now.
> Allen: But I'm not really sure where the project goes from here.
> Jim: Neither am I. I don't think any of us has a real handle on that.
> Allen: I hate not knowing what comes next.

The parallelism of the two passages is striking in its absurdist appreciation of the uncertain. Both move from conviction to a kind of ambiguous unease about the future that Martin Esslin has characterized as "the tragic sense of loss at the disappearance of ultimate certainties" (1987, 416). But although this loss can be disquieting, it can also be liberating, in that it contains within it a hermeneutic intimation of the possibilities of uncertainty. Gadamer points out that "the real power of hermeneutical consciousness is our ability to see what is questionable" (1976, 13). The development of this critical ability, I think, goes to the heart of action research as well as hermeneutics, while its substitution of the question for the answer mirrors Esslin's comment that a key characteristic of absurdist drama is that "instead of being provided with a *solution,* the spectator is challenged to formulate the *questions* he will have to ask if he wants to approach the meaning of the play" (1987, 416).

Revelations of the continuing link between action research, hermeneutics, and absurdism aside, the group's discussions of *Blood and Belonging* made clear the differing interpretations of both nationalism and national identity the group members brought to the work. Although we all held strong opinions about the three texts we read, and despite the fact that, in John Elliott's terms, each group member contributed his "practical wisdom grounded in reflective experiences" (1991, 53), an interesting pattern revealed itself. Those who strongly agreed with Ignatieff's condemnation of ethnic nationalism (Allen and Jim) had similar backgrounds (they were English Canadians whose families had been in Canada for more than three generations). Those who had reservations about Ignatieff's criticisms of ethnically based nationalism (John, Fred, and me) were either ethnic Canadians in a non-traditional sense (neither English nor French) or had some experience of ethnicity that seemed to contradict Ignatieff's blanket dismissal of the concept. John and Fred, in particular, brought an "otherness" to the group that presented ethnicity in terms of resistance to oppression and assimilation rather than as a dangerous precursor to intolerance and xenophobia.

But in addition to bringing to light the growing division within the group over the merits of ethnic nationalism and ethnic identity, our discussion of Ignatieff gradually shifted the focus of the project itself. Rather than centering on nationalism, increasingly we discussed national identity and particularly national identity in its Canadian context. In many ways this shift in focus made sense. We had illustrated most of our discussions about nationalism with Canadian examples and, given the recently failed referendum on Quebec separation, the question of how identity translated into nationalism was very much on our minds and on those of our students. And in our dialogues about *Blood and Belonging* the issue of ethnic nationalism inevitably provoked discussions on the role multiculturalism should play in Canadian nationalism

But concerns about how plural societies establish viable national identities raised the issue of how otherness is dealt with in society in general. Discussing the whole question of "othering" was doubly worthwhile in its educational context. In the educational research community, teachers are frequently the "others": Their voice is seldom heard and it certainly does not carry with it the legitimizing sanction of authority. As is the case with those who have been marginalized, the dilemma of otherness is essentially how to make the stilled voice heard. Action research seeks to accomplish this task through eliminating the distinction between teacher and researcher (Kemmis and McTaggart 1988). In our group, I was acting in the position of mediator, the person who "does not just repeat what he has been told in advance or dictated, [but rather] speaks for the other" (Gadamer in Michelfelder 1989, 51).

Yet in ethnopolitical terms I had also become part of a faction: a faction that had yet another layer of otherness to it. If all teachers have been "de-authorized" in education, teachers like John and Fred have been even more so. Their voices and identities as ethnic teachers have been submerged in the all-encompassing chorus of civic nationalism celebrated in the curricula or they have been submerged entirely through the assimilatory pressures of Anglo Canadian culture. Their embracing of ethnic nationalism as a potentially liberating force perplexed Jim and Allen. That perplexity only increased as we moved on to consider our last reading: Julia Kristeva's *Nations Without Nationalism* (1993).

Act III. The Absurd Implications of Otherness

> I have to speak, whatever that means. Having nothing to say, no words but the words of others I have to speak. (Beckett 1959b, 3)

Language can be a seductive and dangerous thing. In the last thirty years, the neutral view that language is a common medium for transmitting generally understood ideas and for establishing meaning has been subjected to intense scrutiny by poststructural theorists who have rejected the comfortable notion of universality (Foucault 1972; Derrida 1978; Lyotard 1984). In the view of these and other writers, language reflects the presuppositions and cultural assumptions of its traditions; furthermore, it is relational. The meaning of anything is "never knowable purely in and of itself, but only insofar as it bears a relationship to something or to others" (D. Smith 1989, 6). These critical issues that bear on whether meaning in a wider sense can ever really be established emerged with greater frequency as we progressed through the readings, and it was finally our widely differing interpretations over the introduction to Julia Kristeva's work that ended the project.

Kristeva's discussion of the "stranger" within all citizens (1991) represented a definition of nationalism that ultimately focused on the common experience of alienation as a unifying bond for the new nationalism she was proposing. Kristeva's position, that "otherness" (and this meant religious, social, political, and ethnic otherness) needed somehow to be understood and accepted to establish a sense of national identity left the group divided and confused. Allen and Jim agreed that some form of common vision was critical to creating a shared sense of nationalism, but they could not see how this could be achieved if, in Jim's words, "all those 'others' had to be accepted." John had difficulty seeing how otherness could be broader than an acknowledgment of ethnicity and the critical role that acknowledgment played in creating tolerance in multicultural nations. As they explained their positions on the reading, the transformation of the focus of the project that had begun with our reading of Ignatieff continued. Increasingly it was not nationalism we used to illustrate our ideas but national identity. Thus, in explaining his concerns over incorporating otherness, Jim reiterated his preference for civic nationalism as a focus for the identification of the nation's citizens while John emphasized that the plural nature of Canadian society made it imperative to base Canadian nationalism on the concept of diversity and its attendant characteristics of acceptance and toleration.

A common complaint at this stage of the project was that the text itself had become an obstacle to our discussions, but in retrospect it was not so much that Kristeva's ideas presented an insurmountable challenge. The difficulty we were experiencing had more to do with the strong views we had formed and articulated on the nature of nationalism and national identity. And, ironically, the stronger the views became, the less we had to say to one another. Discussing his two one-act plays *The Room* and *The Dumb Waiter,* Harold Pinter noted something very similar to what the research group experienced when he noted that "the more acute the experience, the less articulate its expression" (Pinter in Esslin 1987, 243). In a way, Pinter's comment brought the action research project full circle. Our initial dialogues had carried a sense of common purpose and they had been, by and large, rational and balanced. But over the course of the project we had shed this modernist detachment. Rather than viewing it as an objective concept, we had come to a more subjective appreciation of nationalism, an appreciation that was bound up in our own understandings of national and individual identity.

Ultimately, and perhaps inevitably, our investigation of nationalism took us into the realm of the absurd, and the subjective nature of each of our definitions of nationalism and national identity made communication difficult. This might have been a source of concern for me. After all, we had not answered the questions I had (rather optimistically, as it turned out) asked at the beginning of the project. And I was very much unsure whether our discussion would lead specifically to any improvement in classroom practice. But I found myself curiously unconcerned about the lack of "concrete" results, because what had emerged, both hermeneutic and absurdist in its composition, was another form of understanding. It was the emergence of our "ability to see the questionable" (Gadamer 1976, 13). It was an acknowledgment that, as teachers, we did occupy a location that puts us in a constant state of tension "with the given," whether that "given" was interpreted in terms of differing understandings of national identity or, in a wider context, of the ambiguous position teachers occupy between research and practice.

John expressed this other form of understanding best in a conversation he had with Allen. They had both been arguing over Kristeva's idea that "otherness" had to be included in any workable definition of nationalism. John accepted Kristeva's position that alienation and otherness were a kind of "common denominator" of nationalism, while Allen attempted to make the point that such a definition ignored the mutual desire of groups of people to form themselves into nations. Neither made much headway in convincing the other, but at the end of the session, John looked at Allen and said: "You know, I really can't get the point you're trying to make here, but I understand it's a difficult read and we're both struggling to make sense of the goddamn thing." Perhaps in some small way we had begun to mean something.

Conclusion

But if meaning something in terms of hermeneutic discourse, of absurdist epistemology or of our collective investigation of nationalism was an effective (if somewhat tentative) conclusion to the action research project, unanswered questions still remained. Chief among them were concerns related to the issue of Canadian national identity.

How did we as teachers conceive of Canada's national identity? How had national identity been constructed in the social studies curriculum? If our understanding of nationalism in the post-Cold War era required investigation, even redefinition, was it useful to embark on the same process with national identity?

Closely bound up with these questions, one critical theme emerged from the action research project that helped frame much of this research. That theme was that as teachers, our perceptions of national identity could not exist independently of our own, widely differing, identities. Put more broadly, the questions became: "How is the concept of national identity constructed in plural societies?" and "How is education implicated in this process?" Although many studies on national identity exist, there has been significantly less emphasis placed on what a "curriculum of national identity" should look like in a pluralistic society. When attention has been paid to this issue, it has typically been presented in terms of "official multiculturalism" that does little more than acknowledge overt and "safe" aspects of diversity while it continues to assume the legitimacy of the dominant culture (Giroux 1988, 1993; Mallea 1989; Ghosh and Ray 1987; Ghosh 1996; Hollins 1996).

More recent studies, particularly those written from postmodern perspectives, (Donald and Rattansi 1992; Kanpol and McLaren 1995; Hoffmann 1996; Hollins 1996) tend to examine pluralism much more rigorously. These studies focus on the relationships that exist between groups in a pluralistic society. Rather than providing answers to the modernist question "What is a pluralistic society?," postmodern scholars ask the more open but more problematic question "What does it mean to live in a pluralistic society?," a question that inevitably raises issues of personal, group, and national identities and one that does not automatically assume the likelihood of simple answers. Using the social studies program of Alberta, Chapter 4 takes up these questions through a close analysis of how the curriculum acts to construct Canadian identity.

CHAPTER 4

The Death of the Good Canadian

> In a country with so scattered a population as ours and a vast frontier exposed to alien influences the tasks of creating a truly national feeling must inevitably be arduous but this is the undertaking to which our educational systems must address themselves for by true education alone will the problem be solved. To our schools we must look for the Good Canadian. (Massey in Cochrane and Wallace 1926, 11)

> In 1967 I remember visiting the Centennial Train as a schoolboy. I can remember how excited we were and how proud we were to be Canadian. But I'm not sure that's true anymore. (Jim)

Introduction: The Making of the Good Canadian

Today the fervor of Vincent Massey's appeal to schools to create the "Good Canadian" seems more than misplaced, it carries with it a certain sense of embarrassment: the kind of embarrassment that those who cite Wilfrid Laurier's bold assertion that the twentieth century would be "Canada's century" feel. Like Jim, we have come to view ourselves and our institutions in much more qualified terms. But however out of date it may appear, Massey's evangelistic pronouncement bears close examination for two reasons. First, it theorizes, although it lacks clear definition, the existence of an ideal Canadian type. And second, it explicitly lays out the responsibility of schools for realizing the ideal. In this regard, Massey captured two essential aspects of modernism: the notion of a unique and definable national identity as critical to the survival of the state, and the vital role of the educational system in its manufacture.

This second, functional, aspect of education, particularly of the disciplines of history and social studies, has remained essentially unchanged for more than seventy years. It has determined the curricular parameters used to describe Canadian identity for at least as long. But the modernism that underpins Massey's ringing call to schools deserves careful examination. In the face of what Charles Taylor refers to as Canada's "unresolved national identity" (1993, 111) it is legitimate to ask how schools attempted to construct the Good Canadian, why that attempt failed, and what consequences have resulted from failure. For this reason, an examination of modernism, particularly of its impact on education, is a critical point of departure in any discussion of how and why the current curricula of national identity must be changed.

Modernism and the Invention of National Identity

Modernism as an idea has its intellectual roots in the seventeenth century but reached its height in the nineteenth century. For Albert Borgmann, modernism represents the confluence of the work of Francis Bacon, Rene Descartes, and John Locke and is thus "a fusion of the domination of nature with the primacy of method and the sovereignty of the individual" (1992, 25). In Jürgen Habermas's terms, this confluence was best represented in the Enlightenment Project, which was founded on "the extravagant expectation that the arts and sciences would promote not only the control of natural forces, but would also further understanding of the world and of the self, would promote moral progress the justice of institutions, and even the happiness of human beings" (1970, 98).

In a political sense this sentiment, founded at once on control and progress, found its expression in the idea of the nation-state. Although the modernist idea of nation is essentially a nineteenth century construct, the legitimacy of the concept had been recognized as early as the Treaty of Westphalia, and it began to be realized in the eighteenth century. Beginning with the French Revolution and as an extension of the Enlightenment Project, the nation gradually replaced the monarch as the focus of the people's loyalty, and the idea of the uniqueness of the national character emerged as a basis for the existence of the nation. Thus, Jean Jacques Rousseau, writing in the 1760s could note when discussing the ideal constitution for a nation-state that *"La première règle, que nous avons à suivre, c'est le caractère national: tout peuple a, ou doit avoir un caractère national"* (Rousseau in Cobban 1964, 319).

But Rousseau's hopeful injunction betrays the fragility of the concept in the eighteenth and early nineteenth centuries. Unfortunately for its proponents, the twin ideas of nation and national character were much greater abstractions than the personal embodiment of authority represented by their divine-right antecedents. If Louis XIV could say with some justification *"L'état c'est moi,"* it could be said with equal justification that much of the nineteenth century was taken up with the critical question: *L'état, le peuple, c'est quoi*? But rhetorical questions had little place in the modernist canon of progress, and by the end of the century the answer was clear. The state was the civic nation characterized by the structures most of us have come to take for granted: formalized constitutions, elected legislatures, and written civil and criminal law codes. The people, now become citizens, owed the state their loyalty, while the state, now become the government, owed its citizens protection (Anderson 1995; Gellner 1983).

The nation as political construct and consensual contract between the governed and the governors may have been appealing to political theorists, but it remained a fairly abstract concept. As such it had little hope of earning the enduring loyalty of the people. It was only when government coopted popular, linguistically based nationalism that "modern" national identity emerged in any meaningful sense (Anderson 1995, 109). And ironically, it required the sustaining tension between the Enlightenment concepts of reason and efficiency (embodied in the state) and the less rational but emotively powerful notion of "national character'" (which first emerged in Romantic literary works in the early nineteenth century) to fully realize the potential of national identity. A clear idea of the powerful attraction of romantic nationalism emerges in the works of French historian Jules Michelet. Writing of the particular genius of France, Michelet exults:

> No doubt every great nation represents an idea important to the human race. But great God! How much more true of this is France! Suppose for a moment that she were eclipsed or had perished; the sympathetic bond of the world would be loosened, broken, and probably destroyed. (1973, 183)

But it was neither the abstraction of the nation as "social contract" or the romantic notion of its people as mythic "folk'" that built the modernist idea of national identity. It was the synthesis of the two ideas. Writing in *L'identité de la France,* French historian Fernand Braudel aptly captured this dialectic when he commented:

> *c'est bel et bien d'admettre que la France commence en XVIIIième siècle avec l'époque des Lumières...comme si, dans notre sang, dans notre vie, l'hématologie retrospective ne décelait pas la trace même des lointaines.* (1988, 13–14)

What brought the two ideas together to create a sense of identity and purpose was the machinery of the state itself. Thus, Hegel noted that a "well constituted state" was one in which the "private interests of its citizens coincides with the general end of the state" (1975, 73). But this critical synthesis was achieved only through deliberate action by the state. As Hegel further noted, "For the state to achieve this unity, numerous institutions must be set up and appropriate mechanisms invented" (ibid.). The same observation about the role of the state in the process of national identity formation can be made of Britain. In *The Invention of Tradition,* for example, Marxist historian Eric Hobsbawm comments on "the modernity of what passes for archaic, the manipulated and manufactured character of national ceremony" (1983, 1).

In a functional sense, this dialectic played itself out in the developing educational systems of industrialized nations. As Ernest Gellner has indicated, nationalism relies on the existence of an "education-dependent high culture" (1983, 48–49). In *Peasants into Frenchmen,* historian Eugen Weber notes that the development of patriotism and national sentiment was "the greatest function of the modern school" (1976, 332). Thus national curricula were created to perpetuate, and in many cases manufacture national myths for the twin purposes of grounding national consciousness in some kind of legitimizing historical tradition and garnering the allegiance of the people to the existing political status quo. As Hobsbawm notes, the institutions of the state (and increasingly in the late nineteenth century that meant the educational system) attempted to manufacture traditions for purely self-serving ends. Thus:

> Glory and greatness, wealth and power, could be symbolically shared by the poor through royalty and its rituals. The greater the power, the less attractive, one may suggest was the bourgeois option for monarchy. (1992, 283)

Modernism and Education

Modernist education reflects the function for which it was designed. To the degree that it was created to help realize the Enlightenment Project, its chief attributes remain bound up in the modernist values of control and progress. For Donald Oliver and William Gershman, modernist education is predicated on the need to "improve, ameliorate, develop or assist someone [or something] to mature" (1989, 201). This contention is supported by Henry Giroux who notes that modernist education, and particularly public schooling, is structured to "legitimate an abiding faith in the Cartesian tradition or rationality, progress, and history" (1996, 65). The ends to which this legitimizing process were put were designed to engender support for the existing political status quo and unquestioning acceptance of the capitalist system that was closely associated with the development of liberal democracy in the nineteenth century. Both politically and economically, the aim of modernist education, then, was to manufacture the modern citizen. In economic terms, this end was clearly laid out by American academic Ellwood Cubberly who emphasized that,

> Our schools are, in a sense, factories in which the raw product (children) are to be shaped and fashioned into products to meet the demands of life. The specifications for manufacturing [education] come from the demands of twentieth-century civilization, and it is the business of schools to build its pupils according to the specifications laid down. (1929, 338)

In some ways, the crude functionalism of the economic production model of education has its political equivalent in the state's production of national identity or national consciousness. As Colin Brock and Witold Tulasiewicz conclude in *Cultural Identity and Educational Policy*, the aim of formal education is to shift the focus away from individual identity to allegiance to an "institutionalized cultural identity" (1985, 7). Put more directly, as Rousseau noted, a fundamental end of education was the elevating of students from individual to national consciousness because: *"C'est par elle* [education] *qu'on formera de bonne heure les jeunes citoyens et réunir toutes leurs passions dans l'amour de la patrie"* (Rousseau in Cobban 1964,112).

Modernism and Modernist Education in Canada

What was true of European states in the nineteenth century was essentially true of Canada in its formative period. But assertions of the uniqueness of Canadian national character were tempered by Canada's colonial status. This duality is clearly evident in the attempt of the Canada First movement to promote the development of nationalism in Canada.[1] Thus, while one of the founding members of the movement, R.G. Haliburton, could define Canada's identity in the following terms:

> We are a Northern people-as the true outcrop human nature, more manly, more real, than the weak marrow-bones superstition of an effeminate South. (quoted in Berger 1970, 63)

he could also write of the racial superiority of Anglo Saxon civilization and protest in 1872 against the possibility of disintegration of the empire (ibid., 64).

But if its elites displayed ambivalence toward a uniquely Canadian identity, the critical role they assigned to the institutions of the state in shaping the identity of its citizens showed no such uncertainty of purpose. Thus George M. Grant called upon "the forces inherent in the church, the press, the school, and the college" to aid in the "struggle for national existence" (quoted in Berger 1970, 209).

And if the development of national identity was a critical function of the educational systems of European nations, the same observation could be made of Canada. In 1896, speaking of the threat to national identity posed by massive "foreign" immigration to the Canadian west, a school superintendent warned: "If these [immigrant] children are to grow up as Canadian citizens they must be led to adopt our viewpoint and speak our speech...A common school and a common tongue are necessary if we are to have a homogenous citizenship" (Titley and Miller 1982, 132).

This attempt to manufacture Massey's Good Canadian has had particular significance for Canada and for Canadian education. In many respects it merely encapsulates the modernist attempt to build a national identity that is predicated on building civic consciousness and on creating an emotional attachment to the idea of nation: the sustaining dialectic that I noted earlier. But the very fact of its failure to do so on anything approaching a national scale has elevated the status of the attempt to establish a Canadian identity to mythic proportions and has made schools and school curricula critical focal points in the process.

Inasmuch as education was and remains directly implicated in the modernist attempt to create a "sense of nation," the history of the attempt bears close examination. This examination will focus first on the construction of national identity in the Canadian northwest and subsequently on the idea of national identity in the Alberta *Program of Studies*. Through the course of the analysis I will be arguing that the concept of national identity, itself deformed at its inception, has increasingly become decentered over time. To borrow from poststructural analytical frameworks, national identity, as it has been presented in the curriculum, has become a floating signifier whose meaning is inextricable from the symbolic network in which it is situated (Salecl 1994, 53).[2] But insofar as it still retains its modernist form, it has lost the mythic and emotive power to evoke the passion of students.

The Floating Throne of Byzantium:
Education and National Identity 1867–1914

In his masterful work on the mass psychology of groups, *Crowds and Power,* Elias Canetti discusses the throne of the emperors of Byzantium which, through a series of unseen levers, could seemingly rise and float in the air (1973, 466). The purpose of such a device was clearly to generate awe in the assembled crowds and to demonstrate the magical powers of the emperor. But beyond fairly obvious, if technically sophisticated, demonstrations of power, the psychology of the event is interesting, and it captures much of the nature of the attempt to build a Canadian identity in the period after Confederation. The crowd of retainers were tied to the emperor in a complex relationship that at once both distanced them from the magic of power and bound them to that power. He was the emperor, and they were his subjects, but subject status allowed them to share, however vicariously, in the magic of his rule.

The trope of the floating throne of Byzantium is one that directly applies to the construction of the Canadian identity in the post-Confederation period. Thus, Canadian elites experienced a crisis of legitimacy in which they felt both tied to yet separate from the power and majesty of Britain and the British Empire. Their sense of identity was bound to the conferred magic of the British connection, but that magic was neither duplicable nor was it capable of being transferred, and inevitably, the longer they attempted to sustain the trope, the less likely it was that some other more nationally based trope of identity would develop. The complex nature of this relationship will be explored in the following section, but essentially it will be argued that, along with the federal structure that Confederation brought to Canada, the lack of a strong sense of identity that many Canadians feel today is directly related to events in the post-Confederation era.

In the period after 1867, two critical factors militated against the emergence of a uniquely Canadian national consciousness: the division of powers laid out in the British North America Act and the colonial mentality of the day that placed Canadian nationalism within the context of British imperialism. Related to this last factor was the attitude Canadians displayed to non-British immigrants during the pre-World War One immigration period.

In reference to the first factor, the control of education granted to the provinces by the British North America Act meant, by extension, that a corresponding national curriculum was not developed. Writing in 1919, George W. Ross, first president of the Dominion Educational Association noted that "I have perused with great care the various histories in use in all the provinces of this dominion, and I have found them all to be merely provincial histories, without reference to our common country" (quoted in Chaiton and McDonald 1977, 52).

Robert Stamp makes this same observation.   The relegation of education to the authority of the provinces meant that the opportunity for Canadian schools to "bolster national unity and national loyalty" was lost (Stamp 1977, 32). By the middle of the century, the "regionalization of identity" that George Ross had warned of was firmly entrenched.   In 1943, a committee of the Canadian Education Association examining Canadian history textbooks concluded that "Canadian history is taught not from the national viewpoint, but from the provincial" (Canadian Education Association 1945, 1).

Coupled with what amounted to a constitutionally sanctioned absence of a "national vision" in education, Canada's status as both a colony and member of the British Empire further hampered the development of a sense of national identity. And in this impediment Canadian schools were particularly to blame.

It was perhaps inevitable that Canadians and their institutions would turn toward Britain for legitimacy as they took their first steps toward nationhood; they were already facing a divided nation and the continuing and very tangible threat of assimilation from the United States. This was certainly reflected in education.   Thus, Egerton Ryerson, the prime architect of Ontario's education system in the nineteenth century, could note with approval in 1868: "It is notorious that the attachment of the people to the monarchical system of government and British connection is far stronger now than it was twenty years ago (1868, 6). More specifically, Canada's national identity was specifically linked to its "Britishness." For example, J. A. McClellan, president of the Ontario Teacher's Association predicted Canada's future greatness because "the rich heritage of Britain's history is ours" (1878, 35).

In schools, this association of Canadian identity with imperialism resulted in a curious "synthetic" curriculum that made little distinction between the study of British history and literature and the study of Canadian history and literature. An interesting manifestation of this synthesis is the origin of Empire Day celebrations in English Canadian schools across the country. In 1897, when first approached with the idea of celebrating Queen Victoria's birthday George Ross responded enthusiastically, that he supported "any effort made to foster in our school-children a love for our own country" (quoted in Stamp 1977, 33). Ross's unconscious assumption that imperialism and Canadian identity were synonymous was mirrored in schools and in curriculum until at least the middle of the twentieth century. But as a consequence, schools became active participants in promoting the British connection at the expense of creating a separate sense of nation, and the development of a distinct Canadian identity was severely retarded. Using his own educational experience as an example, historian Arthur Lower has noted: "The wonder is that the tender plant of Canadian nationalism survived at all, for all little Canadian boys and girls have been subjected from the day on which they start school to an unending steeping in the liquid of imperialism" (1958, 350).

This confusion of Britishness with Canadianness had a significant role to play in Canada's reaction to the massive influx of non-British immigrants who played a critical role in populating and developing Western Canada. From 1896 to 1914, more than 3,000,000 prospective citizens immigrated in response to Canadian Immigration Minister Clifford Sifton's call to Europeans to come to the "Last Best West." And although the majority of these new immigrants (1,250,000) came from the United Kingdom, between 1901 and 1921, over 800,000 people whose origin was neither British nor French immigrated to Canada. By 1921, this segment made up fifteen percent of Canada's total population (Palmer, 1975, 7). In the West this "other" immigration had a much more significant impact. For example, in Winnipeg, the proportion of the population who identified themselves as having "British origin" declined from 84 percent to 59 percent between 1881 and 1911 (p. 9). With immigration came the dual issues of cultural accommodation and cultural change. And it can be argued that the governmental response to both issues affected schools and the school curricula in a way that led to a further intensification of the British connection.

In response to the question of how the diverse cultures of the newcomers were to be accommodated, it was decided that aggressive assimilationist policies were the key to the problem that multinational immigration posed to the ethnic balance in the West. Because many immigrant groups tended to settle in blocks rather than in more widely dispersed patterns, this problem was particularly pressing in the eyes of educational officials in the government of the Northwest Territories. In 1898, Northwest Territories' school Superintendent Arthur Goggin noted that the block settlement of the Northwest was "one of the most serious and pressing educational problems for the District." To resolve the problem, Goggin proposed

> to gather the children of different races, creeds, and customs into the common school, and 'Canadianize' them...Though they may enter as Galicians, Doukhobors, or Icelanders, they will come out as Canadians... A common school and a common language will produce that homogenous citizenship so necessary in the development of that greater Canada lying West of the Lakes. (1906, 212–13)

But "Canadianization'" lacked a clear and commonly understood definition. And in the absence of Benedict Anderson's "common imagining," a surrogate was necessary to give substance to the idea of nation. That surrogate was Britishness and the Imperial connection. Both the sense of an "incomplete" Canadian identity and the necessity of assuming some other, more fully developed, identity for the purposes of defining the nation were aptly stated in an *Edmonton Bulletin* editorial in 1892. Writing in response to the developing crisis over whether French-speaking Canadians in the Northwest should be granted the right to operate separate schools, the editor concluded: "This is an English colony until it is something else" ("Editorial," August 15, 3).

A brief examination of the public pronouncements of Canada's elites certainly supports the idea that, in the absence of a strong sense of Canadian identity, it was British identity that was used to both complete and legitimize an incompletely realized national sense of self. In 1905, speaking to the Empire Club of Canada's identity and of its future, E. D. McLaren, general secretary of the Presbyterian Church of Canada noted: "Let us not forget: We too are heirs of Runnymede." He also noted that Canada's continued development as a member of the British Empire would make Canadians worthy heirs of "those principles and traditions that have made Britain's name a name of honor" (McLaren in Titley and Miller 1982, 140). Canada's elites believed that in a public and political sense national legitimacy could be achieved through grafting Canada's identity on to that of Britain; the same hybridity is evident in pre-World War One schools in the West.

I have already mentioned the curious juxtaposition of concepts of British and Canadian nationality evident in the phenomenon of the celebration of Empire Day in schools, and an examination of the curriculum in place in the period before 1914 only serves to confirm the degree to which British and Canadian identity were linked. Students of the day studied British and Canadian history, English literature, and the geography of Canada and the British Empire. The 1898 *Program of Studies* noted that the one of the critical functions of education was the "formation of moral character." This was partly to be accomplished through an examination of the public careers of leading Canadians and Englishmen (Titley and Miller 1982, 143).

Thus the trope of the floating throne of Byzantium was a form of metaphorical trap for Canada's elites. In attempting to legitimize Canadian identity through the conferred magic of the British connection, they effectively froze Canadian nationalism in a colonial mentality that would dominate the discourse on identity for most of the twentieth century. And as the functional arm in the machinery of the construction of identity, schools and the curriculum in the pre-World War One era played a critical role in the institutionalization of this mentality.

The Castle under Siege: 1918–1945

The construction of Canadian identity around the colonial connection was the product of Canada's post-1867 elites. That construction reflected the view that an indigenous national identity was either unrealizable or too weak to withstand the external forces (immigration, American assimilation) that it would have to face (Bercovitch 1993). But despite having to find the locus and legitimacy of national identity in external sources, Canadians still felt a sense of pride and purpose in the attempt. The hybrid messianism of the Canada First movement certainly provides strong evidence of this sentiment. However, in the period after World War One, this sense of purpose began to falter. Rather than focusing on the conscious attempt to build a national identity, there was greater emphasis laid on preserving what had been already built in the face of growing challenges to its survival. In this sense, national identity in the interwar period is centered on the trope of the castle under siege. Certainly schools of the period continued to ground national identity in the British connection. But increasingly, this attempt carried with it a sense of desperation.

In both popular and academic sources it has been persuasively argued that Canadian nationalism was "born" on the battlefields of World War One.[3] But if this was the case in terms of public perceptions of Canada's achievements in the battles of Ypres and Vimy Ridge, it was clearly not reflected in schools or in the school curriculum in the postwar era. The key to understanding why this was the case lies in the progressive entrenchment of cultural diversity in the Canadian west and the growing influence of American culture on Canada as a whole.

Following the cessation of hostilities in Europe, a new wave of immigration reached Western Canada. In its composition, this new immigration was very similar to its prewar antecedent. By 1931, for example, the proportion of the Canadian population whose origin was neither French nor British had risen to more than 18 percent (Palmer 1975, 10). For Canada's public officials and its elites in other spheres, cultural accommodation continued as a critical issue and, as was the case in the period before 1914, aggressive assimilation was the response most often adopted. But again, without a clear sense of Canadian identity, it was almost always the hybrid British/Canadian identity that formed the model to which the newcomers were to be assimilated.

Speaking in a debate over immigration in the House of Commons, R.B. Bennett, federal Conservative leader reinforced this connection by first noting that "the civilization that we call the British civilization is the standard by which we must measure our own civilization" (1928, 3925–27). Having established the parameters of Canadian identity, he went on to warn darkly that in the West:

> In various sections of western Canada they [non-British immigrants] have planted colonies from far-off lands, who have settled upon the soil and maintained their own peculiar civilization rather than become assimilated to that British civilization which should prevail in this country. (ibid.)

Methodist clergyman J. S. Woodsworth, who noted the danger, sounded this same note of warning: "The presence of alien and unassimilated elements" within Canada had retarded the development of a common sense of community within the nation (1972, 86). In an institutional sense, this danger could be met through the school system, whose responsibilities must be widened to provide training in citizenship and in promoting a sense of shared community that emphasized the development of "high political ideals and a 'social conscience'" (p. 89).

What is noteworthy about both commentators' views, apart from the jointly held fear of the foreign "other," is the way in which the two describe Canadian identity. The British model Bennett describes has a clear ethnic identification and implies well-established criteria for the Good Canadian. Woodsworth's prescription is much more vague and relies on the creation of a common set of civic-oriented values as the basis for national identity. Given the fact of increasing pluralism in western Canada, and given the fears this demographic shift engendered in the host society, it was much more likely that the British model, rather than Woodsworth's more broadly based ideal, would continue to be the foundation for teaching Canadian identity in the West.

This tendency to promote the British aspect of Canadian identity was only reinforced by the growing cultural influence of the United States. The strength of this pull was graphically shown by a 1930 survey that showed that among Canadian high school students the seven most popular radio programs were American, and that the same students preferred American over British movies by a margin of two to one (Angus 1938, 369–70). As Robert Stamp has noted of the postwar period: "During these years, Canadian young people substituted American heroes for British heroes, with scarcely a passing thought being given to Canadian heroes. Canadian schools were powerless to halt the trend" (1977, 34).

Fantasizing in School: National Identity and the Social Studies Curriculum, 1918–1945

Faced with the threat of cultural assimilation by the United States, Canadian education remained firmly tied to the Empire, and Canadian identity continued to be framed within an essentially British context. In this struggle for identity, perhaps it was inevitable that, as Robert Stamp has concluded, "Canadian ideals fared a poor third" (1977, 34). The interwar Alberta *Program of Studies* for high schools can be used as a case in point to illustrate Stamp's conclusion. In the final years of public schooling, Canada is only examined in Grade 12 (Social Studies 3), and then as only one of the four themes investigated. Of the other three themes, one is dedicated entirely to a study of "Commonwealth Problems." And in a juxtaposition that was surely more than coincidence, the theme contains far more references to "the Empire" than it does to "the Commonwealth" (Government of Alberta 1939). A further and even more direct example of the failure of schools to elaborate a well-defined Canadian identity can be seen in the 1940 Alberta *Program of Studies for Intermediate Schools*. Although the guide lists among its eight fundamental objectives the need to "develop an appreciation of Canadian culture," it describes in much more detail the intention that students "understand the contributions of explorers, frontiersmen and statesmen to the growth and development of Canada, and the British Commonwealth; and to understand the contribution made by Canada to the trade of the Commonwealth and the world" (cited in Burke 1941, 63). The inability the *Program of Studies* to detail the nature of Canadian culture compared with its description of how the British connection was to be established is telling. It mirrors the failure of schools to develop anything like a well-defined Canadian identity while it highlights the continuing attraction of the reflected power and prestige to be had by associating Canada with Britain and the British Commonwealth.

The nationwide history and English diagnostic tests noted earlier, and commissioned by the Canadian Teachers Federation in 1943, certainly confirm the status Canadian history occupied relative to its British counterpart. Only one of fifteen sections on the examination refers specifically to Canadian history, while nine of the fifteen sections either ask questions requiring students to demonstrate their knowledge of British history or provide students with documents that refer to British history for the purposes of demonstrating students' interpretative and analytical skills (cited in Bussard 1944, 5–24). If even the interpretative framework of assessment could not avoid references to Britain, Arthur Lower's observation, cited earlier, that the development of Canadian identity in Canada's schools was seriously compromised by an overemphasis on the imperial connection certainly holds true.

For Canadian elites, particularly its western elites, the interwar period was a time of evolving crisis for Canada's national identity. Faced with the rapidly changing demographic composition of the Canadian west, the growing cultural influence of the United States, and the increasing remoteness of the British connection, a kind of siege mentality emerged. The net effect of this mentality was a kind of desperate and determined cultural reproduction. In the absence of a fully realized Canadian identity, the Britishness of Canadian identity continued to be stressed. Although giving an indigenous Canadian identity a passing mention, Alberta's schools continued to construct national identity on a foundation that was overwhelmingly British.

1867–1945: The Slow Death of a Fantasy Structure

While it is clearly evident that schools turned to British identity to either legitimize or to support a fragile Canadian identity in the period from 1896 to the end of World War Two, that appeal must be considered to be the result of two key factors over which schools had little control. The first was the changing demographics of the nation. Immigration resulted in the settling and economic development of the west and the expansion of Canada's urban centers, but at the same time it forced Canadian society to examine its own identity in the face of large-scale immigration from countries that were neither British nor French. Because of its own incompletely realized identity and the nativist sentiment prevalent at the time, the British nature of Canada was highlighted to the detriment of the development of a more uniquely Canadian identity. This emphasis on Britishness was intensified by the interwar threat posed by the accelerating influence of American culture on Canada. Just as Canadian society could not avoid these issues, neither could schools. But in both Vincent Massey's terms and in those of other elites of the period, schools had a critical role to play in formulating the Good Canadian. In this role they clearly failed. As taught in schools, Canadian identity continued to occupy the ambiguous space between the increasingly remote, but nevertheless powerful, longing for the glories of Empire and the looming danger of cultural and economic colonization by the United States.

From 1867 to 1945 the tropes that Canada's elites used to construct and sustain Canadian identity proved, in the end, unsustainable, yet the function of schools in the promotion and support of Canadian identity continued. In the period after 1945, schools would still have the mandate to produce the Good Canadian, but increasingly this mandate became a matter of function without form. With national identity progressively emptied of its British content, and, as a result, to a certain degree of its legitimacy, Canada's elites struggled to reinvent Canadian identity in the post-World War Two period. This reinvention implied that schools and school curricula could not separate themselves from the task.

Occupying a Kind of Third Space: National Identity and the Social Studies Curriculum, 1945–1981

For post-colonial theorist Homi K. Bhabha, one of the consequences of imperialism has meant that, in an intellectual sense, colonizing and colonized peoples have been brought together in what he terms the third space a space that is both synthetic and dynamic, one that is "continually in a process of hybridity" (1990b, 210). But this hybridity, Bhabha reminds us, constantly "displaces the histories that constitute it" (p. 211). From this perspective, Canadian identity after 1945 was doubly challenged. Canada's status as a colony and subsequently as a member of the Commonwealth maintained the imperial tie, but increasingly after the Second World War it was American culture and Canada's links to the American economy that came to be Canada's most critical relationship. What amounted to a doubled colonial relationship in turn doubled the problem of hybridity and further problematized the attempt to establish a clear sense of national identity.

But if the result of occupying the third space was a sense of ambiguity in the post-1945 era, then ambiguity, at least in terms of Canadian identity, was given a function and a name. In this sense, the trope of the third space created a kind of opportunity for an identity based on the synthetic, and in response to this opportunity, Canadian political elites evolved the lynchpin theory (McInnis 1969, 587–88). Briefly, the theory held that because of its strong British traditions and given its geographical and cultural proximity to the United States, Canada could act as a kind of diplomatic and cultural middleman between its two more powerful neighbors. The critical role of this position was to translate the culture and diplomatic intentions of Britain to the United States and vice versa. The physical manifestation of the lynchpin theory was the role Mackenzie King had played in bringing together Winston Churchill and Franklin Roosevelt at the Atlantic Charter Conference held off the coast of Newfoundland in 1941. It was a curious invention that served two functions. Indirectly it made a virtue out of Canada's lack of a strong identity, while at the same time it assigned Canada a role that increased its international status. And in many ways it marked the beginning of the creation of Canada's postwar identity that celebrated events external to the nation (Commonwealth membership, UN peacekeeping missions, the cultural attainments of expatriate Canadians, NATO involvement) much more than internal achievements (the building of the Saint Lawrence Seaway System, the construction of the Trans-Canada Highway, the growth of the Canadian Broadcasting Corporation).

The post-1945 school curriculum in Alberta reflected this changed mood to some degree. In both the 1955 and 1965 *Program of Studies* for senior high school social studies, students were expected to undertake an investigation of the Cold War and of the United Nations. In fact, this external set of relationships that characterized Canada's involvement in the postwar world were added to the criteria by which Canada's status as a nation was defined. "Since 1945," the 1955 *Program of Studies* noted, "Canada has played a more significant role in world politics, displaying a sense of responsibility that is the mark of a mature nationhood" (Government of Alberta 1955, 123). What is interesting in the statement is not so much the fact of Canada's growing involvement in global issues but the evident need to contextualize internationalism in terms of nation-building. In taking a role in world issues Canada was displaying the characteristics of "mature nationhood" as much as it was helping to resolve international conflict.

Despite the curricular acknowledgment of Canada's changing role in the global community and the new sense of self that it gave to the Canadian identity, by and large the curriculum continued to ground Canadian nationalism in the political and cultural heritage of Britain. For example, although the 1955 *Program of Studies* for senior high schools made the development of Canada the organizing theme for each of the three different grade levels, in many ways it was an artificial connection. At the grade ten level students examined "The Ancient Origins of Canadian Civilization," but given that students studied prehistory, ancient Egypt, and Mesopotamia, and Greek and Roman civilization, the link to Canada seems tenuous at best (Government of Alberta 1955). At the grade eleven level it was "The Modern Background of Canadian Civilization" that was the focus, but again, the grafting of Canada onto what was essentially a course in early modern and modern European (and particularly British) history seems an awkward hybrid. Just as it had in prewar years, the 1955 *Program of Studies* reserved for grade 12 an examination of Canadian issues from a purely Canadian standpoint. But here again, the context is both imperial and continental. For example, in Unit IV of Social Studies 30, students examine "Nationalism in the Modern World." In the introduction to the unit, the authors note that "The nationalism of various peoples of the Empire was the dynamic creation of the modern Commonwealth" (Government of Alberta 1955, 125).

Viewed from this rather paternalistic perspective, Canadian nationalism remained the product of imperial association rather than the result of any great popular longing for autonomy. The "understandings" set out for the unit further reinforce the sense of the ambiguous nature of

Canadian nationalism. The *Program of Studies* advances the timid observation that "Neither Canada's historical associations with Britain nor her geographic ties with the USA have prevented the building of a Canadian nation" (Government of Alberta 1955, 125).

While the truth of such an observation is demonstrable, the sense of unease—even ambivalence—underlying the entire section seems equally clear. The final "understanding" noted in the section even further bolsters this contingent and tentative sense of nationalism. Having already placed Canadian nationalism uneasily between two superpowers and implying that its creation was the product of the imperial tie, the authors conclude that "the realization of national sovereignty has created problems of internal control and external relationships" (ibid.). Nationalism on its own, then, is presented as somehow suspect. The clear implication is that nationalism for Canada was only acceptable if it was placed within the wider (and fundamentally British) context of the Commonwealth.

But in terms of the role of education in manufacturing the Good Canadian, there hardly can have been a worse set of conclusions. On the one hand, the 1955 *Program of Studies* perpetuated the earlier failure of other programs of study to elaborate what Canadian nationalism or identity was, and in the absence of such an elaboration, it continued to assert that Commonwealth (and essentially British) ties were the basis for Canadian identity. On the other, in problematizing the idea of national sovereignty itself, the *Program of Studies* made it very difficult to investigate Canadian nationalism or Canadian national identity on its own terms.

This failure of successive Alberta programs of Study to delineate the parameters of Canadian identity while at the same time continuing to find a source of national self in the imperial connection was clearly a reflection of the ambivalence its educational elites had toward Canada's colonial status. But in terms of the idea of national identity, this same lack of definition had two unexpected consequences. The first was the diminished faculty to characterize Canada in terms of our difference from "others." Edward Said, writing in *Orientalism*, notes that the construction of national identity "involves the construction of opposites and 'others' whose actuality is always subject to the continuous interpretation and re-interpretation of their differences from 'us'" (1994, 332). Julia Kristeva mirrors Said's contentions when she discusses nationalism in terms of the "cult of origins" that tends to place belonging within the context of ethnic, religious, or historically shared roots (1993, 2). In this regard Canada was clearly deficient.

The second consequence was the opportunity that lack of a well-developed sense of national self presented. Ironically, although the absence of a strong sense of "us" was a problem in terms of the modernist concept of national identity formation, it ultimately led to opportunities for progressive redefinitions of national identity that other nations with much stronger senses of self could not take advantage of.

It is thus arguable that Canada's lack of a strong sense of self, while certainly presenting the modernist idea of nation with a significant challenge, also created the "space" for a much more fluid identity. Recently, writers in both popular and academic spheres have supported this contention. Richard Gwynn, for example, has noted the "transparent" nature of a Canadian identity that he terms "impermanent, mutable, plastic, [and] fragile" (1995, 249). And literary critic Frank Davey calls Canada "a state invisible to its own citizens" (1993, 3). Viewed from this perspective, the same crisis in identity that caused concern on the part of Canada's elite, left Canadians more open to new influences that might influence and alter their perception of who they were. Speaking of the idea of identity Mikhail Bakhtin has noted:

> When there is no access to one's own personal 'ultimate word', then every thought, feeling, experience must be refracted through the medium of someone else's discourse, someone else's style. (Bakhtin in Tiffin and Lawson 1994, 91)

Bakhtin was referring to the idea that individual discourse is always mediated through the filter of others—even if those others are not present. But in terms of national identity formation, this lack of an "ultimate word" implies an openness (Bakhtin would argue an unavoidable relation) to voices outside the self-contained and seemingly autonomous modernist idea of national identity. This openness represents an ambiguous space analogous to Bhabha's third space, and it further implies a constant hybridity. Because of the very lack of national identity that its elites complained of, Canada was much more open than most nations to the rapidly shifting social, demographic, and economic conditions that have become the norm in the last two decades.

Equally critical in the development of the post-1945 concept of Canadian identity was a change in the way society and schools approached multiculturalism. In the pre-World War Two era multiculturalism was generally seen, in an educational sense, in problematic terms. The solution to this dilemma was almost universally assimilation to a Canadian norm. But with successive post-1945 immigrations, first from war-torn Europe and subsequently from non-traditional sites of immigration such as the Caribbean and Southeast Asia, the changing demographic profile of Canada began to assert its own imperative. In 1961, for example, 74.2 percent of the Canadian population identified themselves as having either French or British ancestry. Twenty years later, the census revealed that this proportion of the population had declined to 66.8 percent (Government of Canada 1982).

Ghosts in the Attic: National Identity
and the Social Studies Curriculum, 1945–1970

But this significant change in national makeup was not initially marked by a comparable shift in the Alberta programs of study. While both the 1955 and 1965 guides note as part of the "conclusions" to be reached at the end of the grade eleven theme "Features of Canadian Religious and Cultural Life" that "many ethnic groups have brought with them features which have enriched Canadian life," much more space is devoted to examinations of the Salvation Army, ideological divisions within Protestantism, and the 1924 creation of the United Church of Canada. In terms of Canadian culture itself, the documents remark rather weakly that "since 1900 there have been manifestations of a developing Canadian culture" (Government of Alberta 1955, 110; 1965, 96)

Thus both the 1955 and 1965 programs of study continued the prewar trend to downplay Canadian identity while grounding Canadian culture firmly within a British mold. Where the 1939 *Program of Studies* could speak rather elliptically of the need to develop an "appreciation of Canadian culture" without describing it, in the post-war period students were taught that certain "manifestations" of Canadian culture existed. By comparison, the much more specific curricular references to the evolution and role of church institutions, most of which were firmly British in character, left little doubt that the authors of the Alberta curriculum were quite certain about the religious (and fundamentally British) identity of the nation. In this sense, the two programs of study continued the trend to support the legitimizing role that British identity gave to Canadian identity. Despite their fundamentally colonial mentality, in their references to the role assigned to ethnic groups in Canada, the 1955 and 1965 Programs of Studies do mark a critical intellectual point of departure.

However tentative it may have been, acknowledgment on the part of the curriculum that ethnic pluralism was increasingly a demographic and cultural reality represented the recognition of what has been called the third force in Canadian life (Tarnopolsky 1975). Neither British nor French by birth or ancestry, this third force included visible and non-visible minorities whose racial origins or ethnic backgrounds differed from those of "traditional" Canadian culture. Their entry into the curriculum marked an important first step in what feminist writers have termed the process of becoming visible, but the conditions of their entry also initiated a curricular crisis of representation that remains a central dilemma in the continuing attempt to define the Canadian identity.

In terms of this crisis in representation, the role the curriculum assigned to ethnic minorities in Canada was overwhelmingly contributory and reflected the "emancipatory" tendency in modernist cultures to examine racial and ethnic minorities solely in terms of the perspective of the dominant culture (Giroux 1991; Ghosh 1996; McCarthy 1998). This approach precluded any expression of the perspectives of minority cultures and, in failing to address issues of race and ethnicity in more problematic terms, ultimately marginalized and trivialized both. Thus writing in the mid-1970s, educational historian Manoly Lupul could note:

> We must get rid of what may be termed the "contributions approach," so popular with the Canadian citizenship branch and the United Nations Clubs. This approach is full of name-dropping and statistics, with the emphasis on politicians, scholars, and oat kings. (Lupul in Chaiton and McDonald 1977, 171)

And in a direct response to A. B. Hodgetts's 1968 examination of the state of Canadian Studies in Canada called *What History? What Heritage?* curriculum scholar Ted Aoki and others could write what effectively represented an ethnic minority response to Hodgetts's report, in which they concluded:

> There is an overwhelming British and French cultural perspective within most [provincial] curricula....At the secondary school level...students are encouraged to look at material details relative to ethnic groups or to romanticize about a heritage more often than to grapple with such issues as

pluralism, cross-cultural communication government policy, language and
aboriginal rights, and value conflicts. (1974, 55)

Although in official terms the changing demographic makeup of
Canada was acknowledged by the federal government's adoption of
official multiculturalism in 1971, in terms of how this affected
classrooms and curricula, it was also quite clear that two very different
views of multiculturalism had emerged. On the one hand, from a purely
institutional perspective, the Alberta curriculum was changed to
acknowledge the distinctiveness of Canada's minority cultures and the
significant contributions they have made to the development of Canada.
But on the other, critics have maintained that the way multiculturalism
was examined in schools often led to minority cultures being subsumed
under the dominant culture's ethnocentrism and its modernist
preoccupation with progress and development (Mallea 1989; Ghosh and
Ray 1987; Ghosh 1996; McCarthy 1998).

A Full-Blown Identity Crisis: National Identity and the 1971 Social Studies Curriculum

In some respects, the new values-oriented curriculum that was introduced
in 1971 and that radically shifted the focus of the social studies in
Alberta represented a critical break from its two postwar antecedents. In
other respects, however, it continued to define national identity on
externally based criteria. In terms of a breaking with the past, the most
significant development was the dropping of the British/Commonwealth
connection. For example the 1971 curriculum made the study of Canada
mandatory at grade ten (a restructuring that remains in force today), but
only once in the curriculum specifications was there any reference to
Britain, the Commonwealth, or the Empire. By contrast, in terms of the
three themes of the program that dealt with "Canada External," the
United States figured quite prominently (Government of Alberta 1971,
32-39). But, more critically, the effective replacement of Britain by the
United States as Canada's external point of reference reflected a changed
perception of Canada's national identity.

And Canada's relationship with the United States was presented in
much more problematic terms. References in earlier programs of study
to the "British" character of Canada's institutions and historical
development and to the legitimizing relationship Canada found in the
Empire and subsequently in the Commonwealth did not find their

counterpart in similar references to the role of the United States in Canada's evolution. Instead, the curriculum cautiously inquired how America might react to such policies as non-alignment and placed more emphasis on Canadian political and economic autonomy. When the *Program of Studies* could frankly question whether Canada should move toward non-alignment "if it will affect our friendship with the United States" (Government of Alberta 1971, 38), it seems clear that although the British frame of reference had disappeared, the 1971 curriculum continued the trend of earlier curricula to see national identity in contingent, externally determined, and essentially colonial terms.

But the 1971 *Program of Studies* raised two domestic developments that, increasingly, have played critical roles in how the Alberta curriculum has shaped national identity. The first was the emergence of French-speaking Canada as an ambiguous presence in the curricula. Absent from previous programs of study, the study of French Canadian nationalism was first contextualized in terms of it being a key cause of "national disunity"; yet subsequently the recognition that the Francophone "fact" in Canada had led to official bilingualism was described much more positively as contributing to the "uniqueness of duality" (Government of Alberta 1971, 35–36). To understand the logic underlying the ambiguous representation of French-speaking Canada in the curriculum, it is essential to look at recent examinations of ethnicity and race and how they are dealt with in curricula.

Most studies of schooling and diversity (Hollins 1996; Kanpol and McLaren 1995; Castenell and Pinar 1993; Donald and Rattansi 1992; Brock and Tulasiewicz 1985) express the view that several different models or approaches to diversity exist. But underlying these diverse interpretations, two approaches to the issue dominate the discussion. The first sees diversity in modernist and essentially functionalist terms. Official acknowledgment of diversity is a function of the need to "provide solutions for specific social and educational problems" (Grant and Sachs 1995, 92). From this perspective, it is acceptable for minority cultures to "add" aspects of their own culture to the dominant or common culture in order to accommodate the minority culture's demands for recognition, but these additions are always included on the terms dictated by the dominant culture (Gutierrez and McLaren 1995, 139).

Thus, approving references to bilingualism, in terms of the state-sanctioned, institutionalized identity of Canada emphasized a form of "safe" diversity, one that incorporated linguistic duality into the canon of modernist progress. Writing in *Race, Culture and Difference,* Donald and Rattansi note that statist policies that encourage the incorporation of aspects of a minority culture into a dominant culture (in this case bilingual and immersion schools into the essentially Anglophone education system outside Quebec) represent the "disavowal" that the minority culture can materially affect the values and behavior of the dominant culture. Although such policies as official bilingualism endorse "claims to tolerance and inclusiveness," they remain "within the political logic of assimilation" (1992, 2).

If incorporation of French language education into an English milieu satisfied moderate and federalist francophone desires for recognition, it represented not a significant cultural threat to Canadian identity but acknowledgment that some Quebecers might choose separation as the only way to safeguard their language and culture. And in curricular terms, the programs of study portrayed this latter option as destructive and, by extension, inimical to Canada's national identity. This concern reflects the second approach to diversity, which emphasizes that issues of ethnicity and race must be viewed as a constant series of interactions between dominant and minority cultures and are not infrequently as productive of conflict as they are of tolerance. In their introduction to *Understanding Curriculum as Racial Text,* Castenell and Pinar note that identity is not "a static term...reflective of a timeless, unchanging inner self. Rather, identity is a gendered, racialized, and historical construct...that is, the construction of 'difference,' and negotiated in the public sphere" (1993, 4). The authors further note that minority cultures may, of necessity, view their relations with the dominant culture in terms of opposition and struggle when it comes to issues of identity.

But such perspectives do sit easily with the dominant culture's own image of itself and of its position in society. The modernist idea that differences between the dominant culture and its minorities are simply a "problem" that can be resolved through nothing more than reasoned discussion and "additive" policies dies hard. Thus, the 1971 *Program of Studies* described a critical cause of national disunity as nothing more than a "misunderstanding between the two founding nations" (Government of Alberta 1971, 35). The emphasis on reason as a tool to resolve conflicting and possibly irreconcilable senses of national identity that the statement implies serves as a case in point to illustrate the idea that modernist views of diversity "operate within modes of intelligibility that reproduce the logocentric thinking that reinitiates the logic of domination and oppression" (Kanpol and McLaren, 1995, 13).

The second domestic development having a direct bearing on the idea of national identity and emerging from the 1971 *Program of Studies* was the question of how ethnicity was represented in the curriculum. Viewed much less ambiguously than Francophone nationalism, ethnicity was presented in terms that marginalized and problematized ethnocultural diversity and refused to acknowledge, except in a very negligible way, the growing diversity of Canada's population. Broadly, ethnicity was presented as suspect. Thus "ethnic origins" (of the two founding nations) are presented as a cause of national disunity (Government of Alberta 1971, 36). But when demographic shifts in the composition of Canada's population examined, ethnicity is entirely subsumed under bilingualism and cultural duality. For example, in the section of the *Program of Studies* focusing on whether Canada should have two languages, the "ethnic origin and composition of the Canadian population" and the "assimilation of other minorities in either the English or French linguistic groups" are noted as demographic evidence for the need for two official languages (Government of Alberta 1971, 36).

Canada adopted official multiculturalism in 1971; the irony of the treatment accorded pluralism in the *Program of Studies* is striking. But perhaps this contingent acknowledgment of ethnicity can be explained in terms of the political realities of the day. The emergence of Francophone nationalism on the national scene was, in 1971, a relatively recent phenomenon. While English Canada was still adjusting to the changed vision of Canadian identity suggested by the Official Languages Act of 1969, events in Quebec pushed the political agenda at a much faster pace. The creation of the separatist Parti Québécois in 1968 and the violence surrounding the October Crisis of 1970 introduced the very real prospect of the breakup of Canada. In the face of this crisis, clearly multiculturalism and ethnic diversity fared a very poor second in terms of their treatment in the *Program of Studies*.

The image of Canadian identity as it emerged in the 1971 *Program of Studies* was one of transition and increasing ambiguity. The United States had clearly replaced Britain as the external focus of identity. But although in doing so the ambiguous tradition of nesting national identity in a quasi-colonial relationship was continued, it was a much less comfortable relationship. The reflected glories of the imperial connection were replaced with the less reassuring prospect of living next to the world's greatest economic and military power.   Internally, the emergence of Quebec nationalism as a defining point of identity created an uneasy binary that reinforced the role of the state in manufacturing national identity at the same time that it introduced the possibility of the fragmentation of the nation itself.   But in "fixing" Canada's internal identity around the conflict and accommodation basic to the historical relationship between English and French Canadians, cultural pluralism disappeared as a model for national identity except as it could somehow contribute to the "uniqueness of duality" noted earlier.

   The transitional nature of the 1971 *Program of Studies* confirmed the notion of the hybridity of national identity in the curriculum.   It also reinforced the notion that, in the curriculum, national identity was to be found in the third space between two originary cultures.   In 1971, however, the location of this space shifted dramatically.   Rather than existing in the interstices between Canada's British heritage and its Americanized economy and culture, national identity was to be found increasingly in the cultural interplay between French-speaking and English-speaking Canadians.   But in modernist terms, the lack of resolution of the "problem" of Quebec and increasing concern over the failure to produce a fully realized national identity created a crisis atmosphere in education that ultimately spelled the death of the idea of the Good Canadian and problematized the modernist notion of national identity itself.

Edging Nervously toward Pluralism: National Identity and the 1981 Social Studies Curriculum

A decade later, the 1981 Alberta *Program of Studies* continued the trend, begun in 1971, to focus Canadian identity on the evolving relationship between French and English Canada.   Thus under the theme "Canadian Unity," the curriculum suggested that students study "issues of cultural control in Quebec in the 1970's," "issues of political separation in Quebec in the 1970's," and "issues of bilingualism in Canada in the 1970s" (Government of Alberta 1981, 77).   By comparison with the 1971 curriculum, however, there was a growing acknowledgment that national unity was, at least partly, a reflection of difference.   While the 1971 curriculum could view national unity in terms of a fixed set of problems requiring a no less rigid set of solutions, the 1981 curriculum noted that "in nations like Canada where geographic, cultural, and economic differences exist, striving for an acceptable form of national unity leads to continuous readjustments of power between different levels of government" (p. 77).

The key term in the generalization was "acceptable" in that it implied that national unity, and by extension national identity, was not a matter of adherence to universally accepted and understood norms but was, instead, a function of consensus, dialogue, and discussion. But it is also interesting to note that, in keeping with the modernist idea of national identity, this dialogue was clearly to take place at the governmental level. Such a perception maintained the nineteenth-century concept that the state, and the state alone, was responsible for the manufacture of national identity. As Homi Bhabha observes: "the first duty of the state is to 'give' to the nation its cultural identity, and above all to develop it" (1995, 178).

But in the case of the 1981 *Program of Studies,* the "gift" of identity remained problematic at best. In functional terms, there was ample evidence to support the contention that governments were assigned the role of resolving the question of national unity and delineating the parameters of the national identity. However, given the lack of a clear sense of self and in the face of an ambiguous understanding of English Canada's relationship with French Canada, it appears that the curriculum's tentative and hopeful conclusion that an "acceptable form" of national unity existed was all that could be expected.

The treatment of multiculturalism in the 1981 curriculum continued the subordinate status it was assigned in the 1971 *Program of Studies*, but the location of its dependency shifted in 1981. Although the curriculum developed the concept of "identity" in a section on Canadian unity, no references to ethnicity, multiculturalism, or diversity were made in the section. Instead, in a later section dealing with "Canada and the World," brief references were made to the emergence of a "cultural mosaic" as one of the consequences of Canadian immigration policy. In terms of its representation, ethnocultural diversity was virtually absent from the 1981 *Program of Studies*, and when the issue of diversity was broached (in very restricted terms), the clear implication was that Canada was characterized by a high degree of cultural uniformity.

Opening Up the Third Space: National Identity
and the Social Studies Curriculum, 1955–1981

It is clear that from 1955 to 1981 the themes of transition and ambiguity marked the four programs of study issued during the period. As the relevance of the British model diminished, concern began to be expressed about the exact nature of Canada's relationship with the United States. At the same time, the emergence of French Canadian nationalism presented a direct challenge to English-speaking Canada's comfortable images of domestic peace and national unity. And all the while the as yet unresolved issue of the significance of the rapidly changing demographic composition of the nation was beginning to make its influence felt. Given these seismic shocks to Canada's national identity, the "them-us" binary that is so characteristic of modern nationalism (Spivak 1985; Kristeva 1993; Salecl 1994; Mouffe 1995) remained undeveloped. Psychologically, then, there was no "final word" in terms of Canada's national identity (Lacan in Zizek 1989, 131) that froze national identity in the realm of the symbolic. Instead, a shifting series of responses—to the loss of the imperial fantasy; to the more threatening colonial relationship with the United States, to the rise of Francophone nationalism; to the undeniable fact of growing pluralism— left the terrain of national identity ambiguous and uneasy ground. This ambiguity and unease emerged full-blown in the 1990 version of the *Program of Studies.*

The Ambiguous Possibilities of the Third Space:
The 1990 Social Studies Curriculum

It was at this critical juncture that the Alberta *Program of Studies* displayed both the flaws and the possibilities inherent in the trope of the death of the Good Canadian that has been the focus of this chapter. The modernist vision of national identity, a vision founded on the uniqueness of the "national character" yet ironically dependent on the state for its creation and continued renewal, had proven untenable in the face of the conditions of ambiguity and transition that characterized Canada and Canadian classrooms in the post-1945 period. But if the content of the message had been substantially invalidated, the form of its delivery remained unchanged. This disjunction between the form of a modernist curriculum and growing irrelevance of its content produced a sense of tension within the curriculum, but it also produced opportunities for other, more fluid, understandings of national identity to emerge.

As was the case beginning in 1971, the 1990 *Program of Studies* mandated grade ten as the last year for an intensive study of Canada. The curriculum guide set out three interconnected themes for examination: sovereignty, regionalism, and identity (Government of Alberta 1990). But the 1990 guide represented a clear departure from the postwar guides that preceded it in its focus on Canadian identity. Students were encouraged to "assess the importance of Canada developing a strong national identity" and to take up the problematic question "What is the Canadian identity?" (Government of Alberta 1990, 9). And unlike the programs of study that preceded it, the parameters of national identity were not only hinted at, they were defined in a much clearer fashion. Canadian identity, the guide specified, was a product of four specific forces: identification with community, region, and nation; the communal values, attitudes, and cultures that have emerged from our history and geography; official state-supported bilingualism and multiculturalism; and group interaction (Government of Alberta 1990, 13–14).

When examining the four bases of Canadian identity, it is interesting to note that two of the four deal with the ongoing process of identity formation (the evolution of values, attitudes, and cultures and group interaction), while the remaining two bases of identity define the parameters within which Canadian identity develops (community, regional, and national identification and bilingualism and multiculturalism). But given that the elaboration of the first parameter (community, regional, and national identification) is limited entirely (and curiously) to references to an examination of "how others perceive Canadians" it is difficult to conclude that much importance was assigned to this aspect of national identity (Government of Alberta 1990, 14). The case of the importance given to bilingualism and multiculturalism was much different. Both concepts were described as "fundamental to the Canadian identity" and references to them as "our official policies" further sets them apart from the other bases of national identity by adding the sanction of the state to their status (p. 14).

The emergence of multiculturalism from its subaltern status further marked the 1990 curriculum as significantly different from its antecedents. No longer subsumed under bilingualism or Canada's international interactions, the 1990 *Program of Studies* presented multiculturalism in terms that acknowledged the undeniable "fact" of pluralism while at the same time presenting some of the key issues that attended cultural diversity. For example, under the concept "cultural identity," assimilation, cultural maintenance, and cultural promotion were discussed, and under the theme "nationalism," pluralism was described (albeit rather vaguely) in terms of a "value" that Canadians hold (Government of Alberta, 1990, 14). But if the 1990 curriculum represented an acceptance of increasing pluralism, and if it attempted to make an examination of Canadian identity an important component of grade ten social studies, it must also be said that the terms of that investigation link the 1990 *Program of Studies* firmly to the modernist paradigm. In this sense, it continued the attempt to define the Good Canadian that was typical of the curricula that preceded it. A careful reading of the Identity section of the curriculum reveals both its modernist thrust and the reasons for its failure to engage the passions of students.

A Conversation with the Curriculum

As with the other themes, the expectations that formed the basis of the identity section were clearly and prescriptively laid out. But in terms of the broader question of identity formation, these same expectations created what amounted to an impersonal checklist of national characteristics. The curriculum established a rigid and imposing structure of national identity that allowed for little flexibility in response to changing local, national, and global conditions. Such a sterile listing cannot possibly produce the "emotive power of a sovereign community" (McCrone 1992, 6) that is at the base of nationalism's attraction.

In four short prescriptive statements, the *Program of Studies* effectively excluded students from exploring their own understanding of national identity. Thus a student with the *right* sense of identity is one who empathized with: "community, region, and nation," understood that Canadian identity was "shaped by our values, attitudes and cultures as they have emerged from our history and geography," believed "that bilingualism and multiculturalism are fundamental to the Canadian identity," and could appreciate that "interaction among groups influences one's identity" (Government of Alberta, 1990, 13–14).

It was not that these characteristics were somehow outdated or "wrong." Together they formed the basis for what was clearly intended to be a civic culture founded on humane and empathetic values, but significant questions must be asked about the modernist design of the section itself. The most crucial of these deals with the failure to engender what Renata Salecl has termed the "fantasy structure" of the nation (Salecl 1994, 15), in which it is possible for individuals to identify with the nation as a symbolic and unifying construct. In Benedict Anderson's terms, this fantasy structure has an emotive element, which he refers to as "a deep horizontal comradeship" (1995, 7), but it is nevertheless a symbolic space that overcomes barriers of distance and time such that "members of even the world's smallest nation will never…meet [nevertheless] in the minds of each lives the image of their communion" (p. 6). Ironically, the emotion, fantasy, and sense of communion that Salecl, McCrone, and Anderson refer to were arguably present in most pre-WW I curricula, but two factors made this fantasy untenable in late twentieth-century Canada.

The first was the fundamentally unrepresentative nature of the fantasy itself. Over time, as demographic changes and broader cultural influences affected the Canadian population, the post-Confederation "Britishness" of Canada became increasingly irrelevant. Perhaps even more importantly, the manufactured nature of modernist national identities contributed to the growing irrelevance of the fantasy. As Leah Greenfeld writes, "There are no 'dormant' nations which awaken to the sense of their nationality…rather invention and imposition of national identity lead people to believe that they are indeed unique and as a result to become united" (Greenfeld in Corse 1997, 22). But the "invention and imposition" Greenfeld discusses implies an external power providing or mandating the "gift" (in Homi Bhabha's terms) of a national identity. And as the legitimacy of the state itself was increasingly questioned (Barber 1995; Taylor 1991; Borgmann 1992; Lasch 1984) in the latter decades of the century, so was the externally sanctioned "gift" of a national identity.

But the modernist notion that there are fixed referents of national identity and that these referents are somehow tied to a common experience or imagining of Canadian history fits well into Benedict Anderson's assertion that modern nations must be imagined communities. In this regard, and perhaps most critically, the *Program of Studies* identified bilingualism and multiculturalism as "fundamental to the Canadian identity." The identification of these twin pillars of identity further linked the Alberta social studies curriculum to the tenets of nineteenth-century nation-building. It is arguable that "official" bilingualism and multiculturalism were creations of the federal government, and in this sense they fit the definition that modern national identity is a construct of the state. And, in theory, the two also create a mythic structure that allows for a more emotive attachment to the idea of nation. As is the case in most nations, this mythologizing begins with schools and the curricula they teach (Weber 1976; Callan 1994). However, a brief examination of recent attempts to create a mythic structure of national identity reveals the failure to create anything like a "common imagining" of the nation.

Chronicle of a Death Foretold:
Failed Attempts to Manufacture the Myth of the Good Canadian

From A. B. Hodgetts's 1968 nationwide survey of student attitudes toward their country to Chaiton and McDonald's 1977 investigation of the record of Canadian schools in promoting national identity to the Alberta government's own 1981 Canadian Awareness Project, to J. M. Granatstein's recent work, *Who Killed Canadian History?* (1998), a significant amount of attention has been paid to ministering to the needs of the ailing Canadian identity in our schools in the last thirty years (Hodgetts 1968; Chaiton and McDonald 1977; Government of Alberta 1981). In almost all similar studies (and certainly in the specific instance of the four works cited), a sense of desperation pervades the findings. Hodgetts, for example, spoke in urgent terms of the need to exploit the "fresh new spirit" of Canada's Centennial to build a "more rational political community, approximating the democratic ideal" (1968, 122). The conclusions of the Canadian Awareness Project were much more apocalyptic. Pronouncing itself "dismayed" by student scores in the grade twelve history component of the diagnostic examination it administered, the committee responsible for the exam warned that the evident lack of understanding of Canadian history displayed by graduating high school students could "inhibit a person's ability to develop a sense of national identity" (Government of Alberta, 1981, 227).

Sixteen years later neither the sense of dismay nor the modernist approach to national identity had fundamentally changed. In June 1997 the *Edmonton Journal* reported the results of a national survey of the historical literacy of Canadians aged 18 to 24. The survey noted with alarm the national average score of 34 percent on the thirty questions assigned and the Dominion Institute, the sponsors of the questionnaire, warned that the lack of knowledge of Canada's history meant that Canada's youth lacked the "cultural currency" that was critical to the development of a national identity. As a prescription for remedying the crisis, the Institute recommended a mandatory history course in each province that would include "a minimal list of people and events" critical to Canadian history ("Dominion Institute Releases," June 20, 2000, p. A 14).

Periodic calls for either provincial or national crusades to rescue and reinvigorate Canada's national identity aside, in terms of the quest for the Good Canadian, it is apparent that by the late 1960s the sense of mission that guided the search had begun to founder. Although it was possible for Robert Laxer to echo Vincent Massey and to speak of the unifying bonds of "our search for an English-speaking identity" (1969, 113), implicit in his statement was that the goal itself had been abandoned and that English Canadians were united only in the quixotic attempt itself. Even more telling was Hodgetts's conclusion that "it is both futile and undesirable to search for it [national unity] in a vast, multi-ethnic country like Canada" (1968, 119). Given the sense of pessimism and urgency that pervades his 1968 work, it is interesting to compare these sentiments with those he expressed in *Teaching Canada for the 80's* published exactly ten years later. While references to the goal of achieving national unity have been replaced with the aim of realizing the much more diffuse concept of "pan-Canadianism" (Hodgetts 1978, 1–8), a closer examination of the text reveals the same sense of disillusion that was present in 1968. Hodgetts and his co-author Paul Gallagher note:

> In 1968...the author of *What Culture? What Heritage?* predicted precisely the situation that now exists...The prediction was made to encourage our educators to break out of their provincial cocoons and see the national needs; it was hoped that they would realize that schools might help meet these needs by eliminating some of the abysmal ignorance and misunderstanding that exists between peoples from different regions and from differing linguistic, ethnic, and cultural backgrounds. It is apparent that this challenge has not yet been faced. (1978, 131)

By the middle of the next decade, however, there was an entirely different response to the "challenge" that Hodgetts had referred to seven years earlier. In the 1985 compilation *A Canadian Social Studies,* the issues of national identity and Canadian unity are barely noted. Instead, what emerges is a volume dedicated to the *technique* of teaching social studies as it applies to Canadian classrooms. Of the eighteen articles that make up the text, only one, a survey article, deals with Canadian content in the social studies (Parsons, Milburn, and van Manen 1983). This emphasis on methodological concerns implies two complementary trends, both of which have implications for the teaching of national identity in social studies classrooms. In the first case, the emphasis on methodology at the expense of content merely confirms the tendency, noted earlier, to abandon the search for a single Canadian identity. But the focus of the work on approaches to social studies stressing skills development, problem solving, and critical thinking, all under the general theme of developing "responsible citizens," may well represent what George Tomkins refers to as education critical to allow students "to cope effectively in a pluralistic society" (1977, 20).

Intellectually, *A Canadian Social Studies* marks a significant point of departure in terms of the issue of Canadian identity. The ease with which it presents differing approaches to teaching social studies without the attendant references to the need for a "common imagining" that mark Hodgetts's work imply a kind of benign and essentially unproblematic understanding of the plural nature of Canadian society. But at the same time, the approach the authors take to teaching social studies in Canada further problematizes the idea of a fixed national identity. In their introduction to Part One of the text, for example, the editors note that "It may be that the development of personal and social relationships with other students can be expanded to include wider communities and, ultimately, nations" (1985, 1).

But this conditional acknowledgment that the development of national consciousness *might* be a consequence of social studies education is very far from Massey's 1935 injunction to schools to create the Good Canadian.

Conclusion

It seems clear that in some critical ways Hodgetts, Gallagher, and others had anticipated the crisis that faces social studies at the beginning of the twenty-first century. Their doubts about the role of schools in preserving and strengthening national identity betray a growing uneasiness about the modernist project as a whole. And underlying the urgent tones and the dire warnings is the unstated, but no less real, concern that the dream of nation may be unattainable. Certainly the confident sense that Canada was a "nation in the making" (Cook, Ricker, and Saywell 1964, 52) has recently been challenged by views of national identity that question the sense of purpose and optimism that characterize modernist definitions of the term. Sacvan Bercovitch, for example, calls Canada "a country with a mythology elsewhere, systematically de-centered, and characterized, accordingly, by a rhetoric of absence" (1993, 6). And Alan Sears has written "Canadians are and always have been a people of divided loyalties with multiple understandings of the country and their relationship to it" (1996–97, 61).

Social studies teachers cannot isolate themselves from these concerns. The debate over what our national identity is and how it should look in the future has direct implications for what we do in the classroom. From personal and sometimes frustrating experience it seems clear that the modernist concept of constructing a universally accepted national identity is problematic at best. At the same time, it seems equally clear that students need *some* sense of community and shared experience in their lives.

This sense of community is critical. In the absence of community, modernism risks degeneration into what Albert Borgmann terms the cancerous state of individualism in which people live "in a state of narcissism and pursue loneliness" (1992, 3). Charles Taylor calls the same phenomenon "hypertrophy," a condition in which the modernist emphasis on individualism produces a form of "total emptiness, in which nothing can be recognized any more as of intrinsic worth" (1993, 60). Whether it is termed narcissism or hypertrophy, it is worth noting that there is a significant danger to a society when its citizens lose their emotional attachment to that society. As Eamonn Callan notes: "Civic virtues entail distinctive emotional engagements in the ongoing life of a political community, and politics in a society in which public emotions have largely atrophied will tend to become a matter of apathy and cynicism" (1994, 191).

The issue, then, is to reexamine how we teach national identity in the face of changing conceptions of what it means to be a member of a nation state. This reexamination is critical if schools are to continue to be viewed as having a meaningful role to play in the development of national consciousness.

The action research project that we embarked on was an attempt to respond to this issue and it returns us to Jim's comment at the beginning of this chapter. In the face of the death of the modernist idea of the Good

Canadian and given the hybrid and transitional third space that Canadian identity has come to occupy, what are the possibilities for a reimagination of national identity within the social studies curriculum? Chapter 5 will take up this question in much greater depth.

CHAPTER 5
Reimagining the Good Canadian

> When I first came to this country, in many ways it seemed as British as India. But now things are changing rapidly. Immigration seems to be creating a new kind of Canada.
>
> —Sunita

Introduction: Ambiguity as Opportunity

In a subject area that remains overwhelmingly male and European, Sunita's comments represent an important starting point for reconceptualizing the teaching of national identity. Thus, as a social studies teacher who is also a woman and a member of a minority, she speaks for the other that has frequently been silenced in curriculum discourse. In one sense her comments mark the death, discussed in Chapter 4, of the modernist idea of the Good Canadian. In another sense, they open up the whole question of the relationship of ambiguity to identity and point to the difficulty of fixing Canadian identity in an era of rapid change. Finally, they raise the issue of the role of education in the construction of national identity.

As a classroom social studies teacher, Sunita found herself ambiguously situated between that older, modernist identity and the shifting terrain of contemporary national identity she had tentatively mapped out. For her and for social studies teachers like her, the question of what national identity means in a plural society represents a dilemma that has both philosophical and practical importance. This dilemma situates teachers between what the curriculum mandates in terms of the study of national identity and the experience of identity that their students bring to the classroom. It further locates teachers in an indeterminate space in which their own identities and understanding of national identity increasingly play a critical role in how they approach teaching national identity.

In an intellectual sense, curricular representations of national identity have created their own kind of third space in which the *Program of Studies* assumes the role of the colonial power, while teachers and students represent colonized peoples. The resultant interface between the two creates the ambiguous space that Homi Bhabha (1990b) referred to as a hybrid and shifting location. In terms of the location that classroom teachers occupy, the analogy is both pertinent and accurate. But it also represents the opportunity that ambiguity and uncertainty can provide. Raymond Williams writes that when the dominant culture is disrupted, it is less able to recognize (and by extension suppress) alternative "political and cultural meanings" (1981, 43) Discussing this same ambiguity or deformity, Bhabha (1995) also notes the freedom that is both implied and promoted by "indeterminacy."

In many ways, Chapter 5 is an investigation of whether classroom teachers can take advantage of the opportunity that indeterminacy and ambiguity provide to reimagine the Good Canadian.

Orchestrating Ambiguity

As I note in Chapter 3, questions about national identity had emerged from the earlier action research project in which teachers reexamined their conceptions of post-Cold War nationalism that led to a broader project. From that first group, three original participants expressed an interest in continuing their collective reflection on their teaching practice as it related to national identity. Two other participants joined the group to make six members in all (including me). We agreed to meet regularly to discuss the issues and texts we had agreed on. We further decided that our discussions should be taped and that I would transcribe these tapes and present the transcriptions from time to time for the group to validate and if necessary, clarify.

Collectively we also set a tentative agenda for the project. We decided to begin with a general discussion of our own understandings of the meaning of national identity. We intended to focus next on an analysis of the treatment accorded national identity in the 1990 Alberta *Program of Studies*. Following this, with the help of two texts—Charles Taylor's *Reconciling the Solitudes* (1993) and Patrick Slattery's *Curriculum Development in the Postmodern Era* (1995)—we intended to examine new ways to imagine national identity and construct a curriculum of national identity. Finally, we proposed to use the results of our discussions to attempt to redesign exercises on Canadian identity in an effort to make them more relevant to the classroom settings we worked in and to discuss, evaluate, and revise these exercises based on our perceptions of how well they succeeded in the classroom.

In setting these parameters for the project we were conforming to traditional approaches to action research. The stages of action research that Altrichter, Posch, and Somekh describe as "finding a starting point, clarifying the situation, developing action strategies, and putting them into place, and analysis and theory generation" (1993, 9) were all present in the agreed-upon plan. The structure of our action research project matched Kurt Lewin's action research spiral that consists of "analysis, fact-finding, conceptualization, planning, execution, more fact-finding or evaluation; and then a repetition of this whole circle of activities" (Lewin in Sanford 1988, 127). And, in that we were concerned with changing our teaching practice, we were certainly obeying Stephen Kemmis's injunction that research should be used as a tool for "improving (simultaneously) both practice and knowledge about practice" (1988, 36).

But as I have already indicated, both the concept that we had chosen to investigate and the lived classroom experience of the participants were bound up in ambiguity. Thus the instrumentalist preoccupation with technique and method that characterizes practical action research orientation (Taba and Noel 1988; Sanford 1988; and Altrichter, Somekh, and Posch 1993) was not particularly appropriate to this study.

More suitable to the doubly ambiguous location of this research is a poststructuralist orientation in which action researchers examine "the ambiguities, tensions and conflicts in our own understanding of ourselves, and others; as well as the language within which all such matters are cast and sedimented" (Houtekamer, Chambers, Yamagishi, and Good Striker 1997, 139). Grounded in the notion that "teachers' self-understandings of their practices can alone constitute a source of critical self-reflection and emancipatory action" (Elliott 1991, 116), poststructuralist action research takes up issues of ethical obligation and ecology. For Carson and Sumara poststructuralist action research is conceived of as *a living practice* that demands "that the researcher not only investigate the subject at hand but, as well, provide some account of the way in which the investigation both shapes and is shaped by the investigator" (1997, xiii). Ironically, such a requirement, because it could be applied to both the conceptual indeterminacy surrounding national identity and to the ambiguous environment in which our action research plan was carried out, conforms to traditional approaches to action research and represents what Altrichter, Somekh and Posch (1993) have termed an effective starting point for the project.

Part I: The Past Is a Different Country

Mais, quand d'un passé ancien rien ne subsiste, après la morte des êtres...seules, plus frêles mais plus vivaces...l'odeur et la saveur restent.... a se rappeler...l'édifice immense du souvenir. (Proust in Matore and Eristov 1980, 53)

For Proust's Monsieur Swann, the past was implied in the present. An odor or a taste had the power to evoke an earlier, and in this case, more idyllic period. This same Proustian sense of nostalgia underlay our initial discussion of national identity.

In the *Invention of Tradition,* Hobsbawm and Ranger (1983) argue powerfully that national character and the traditions that it celebrates are largely self-serving constructs of the state. From this perspective, any sense of nostalgia or longing for the past must necessarily be an act of self-deception, but from our initial meeting, it was nevertheless clear that our perceptions of national identity were conditioned by nostalgic associations.

The central metaphor around which this nostalgia organized itself was Canada's 1967 Centennial and the Centennial train that had crossed the country providing hundreds of thousands of school children with what became a powerful and enduring image of national identity.

Jim was the first to use the image. We had agreed that our inaugural session would focus on our understanding of the meaning of national identity, and after several unsuccessful attempts to define it in terms of essentially modernist parameters (government-sanctioned bilingualism, multiculturalism), Jim conjured up the Centennial and how it made him feel proud to be a Canadian. Most of the rest of us agreed. Our experiences of Canada's Centennial celebrations had an emotional aspect that conveyed both a sense of deep personal pride and a shared sense of community. Writing in *Imagined Communities,* Benedict Anderson (1995) aptly captures this experience when he reminds us that modern nationalism must be read *genealogically,* "as the expression of an historical tradition of serial continuity" (Anderson 1995, 195).

For four of the six members of the group, the Centennial, and more particularly the Centennial train, itself a powerful Canadian archetype, represented Anderson's image of "serial continuity." Mutual recognition of this metaphor, even thirty years after the event, still had the power to generate Proust's *édifice immense du souvenir* and, more importantly, it matched Jay Hubbell's thesis that in nations such as the United States and Canada, which lacked the "assumed congruity" typical of the relationship between the state and its peoples in Europe, it was absolutely critical that "traditions be provided and the sentiment of nationality kindled" (1972, 10). Here, then, was an example of both the artificiality of tradition, as Hobsbawm and Ranger viewed it, and the nostalgic power of that tradition, artificial or not, to establish a shared sense of national identity.

The Personal Dimensions of Otherness

But it was curious to note that none of us could find an event subsequent to 1967 that generated a similar sense of communion, and in the discussion that followed what emerged were significantly different narratives of the event itself. For Fred, ethnically German, the Centennial was the definitive rupture with the British model of Canadian identity. Reflecting on both his past and that of his family, who had experienced harassment and ridicule for their German origin in World War Two, Fred noted: "That's when I really began to feel Canadian, After 1967, we weren't British anymore. I think it's when we grew up as a country." When others, notably Jim, remarked that the British connection could not simply be discarded as an aspect of Canadian identity, Fred noted with a bitterness that surprised the group, "That's your Canada, that's your history; it's not mine."

At this point, John, a Ukrainian Canadian, told a story of a 1938 vice-regal visit to his childhood home in central Alberta. He noted how all schoolchildren had spent the previous weeks mapping out the royal itinerary in red thread on a map of Canada and how they were instructed how to act when the Governor General was introduced to the crowd. While relating the enthusiasm of the moment, he indicated with some irony that the patriotic sentiment expressed at the time did not stop his uncle from being interned as an enemy alien during the Second World War.

For John, as it had for Fred, the Centennial had represented a kind of liberation from a colonial model of national identity that had effectively excluded them on the basis of their own (unacceptable) ethnicity. Writing of this exclusivist definition of national identity, Julia Kristeva discusses the "cult of origins" that she classifies essentially as a "hate reaction" predicated on, *"Hatred of those others* [Kristeva's italics] who do not share my origins and who affront me personally, economically, and culturally" (1993, 2–3).

This same sense of the tendency of national identity to be based on the need for a foreign "other" has already been noted in the work of Edward Said, but in Kristeva's work the process of othering takes on a much more menacing tone than it does in Said's *Orientalism.* Kristeva's acknowledgment of the chauvinism underlying modernist national identity is supported in Renata Salecl's observations about the psychological dimensions of the phenomenon. She writes,

> national identification with the nation ("our kind") is based on the fantasy of the enemy, an alien who has insinuated himself into our society and constantly threatens us with habits, discourse and rituals which are not "our kind." (1994, 20)

The revelation that both John and Fred felt a sense of otherness tied to their ethnicity and to the hostility and distrust their families had experienced at the hands of Anglo Canadian society and that this sense of exclusion had played a role in the symbolic significance they assigned to the Centennial jolted the group out of the collective nostalgia that initially marked our discussion of the events of 1967.

And it was an important reminder of the ease with which the "unitary discourse" of Western society made individual and minority identities invisible in the face of the experience of the dominant culture (Foucault, 1980, 86). But these displaced histories in the form of anecdotal accounts from the margins of "national history" comprised a critical aspect of John and Fred's sense of identity. In fact, their reemergence represented an important act of self-assertion that posed difficult questions for the concept of national identity as an act of "common imagining." In response to this kind of indeterminacy, Sunita expressed the concern that if even such generally celebrated and apparently commonly understood symbols of national identity as the Centennial could be interpreted in widely diverging ways, "there might not be anything that we could agree upon as making up national identity." Her concern over what we could "agree upon" had a broader significance than the question of how to create a consensual list of symbols of national identity. For some members of the group, John and Fred's stories raised doubts about the ultimate validity of universal symbols of national identification.

But not for all members of the group. The perceptions of Fred and John of the Centennial as an act of distanciation from a colonial and racial past was not matched by the perceptions of Jim and Peter, both Anglo Saxons and quite proud of their British heritage. For them, the Centennial had been a celebration of a century of achievement that was inextricably tied to the establishment in Canada of British parliamentary institutions, British culture, and the reflected glories of imperial and subsequently Commonwealth ties. From their perspective, Canada's national identity was reinforced, not diminished, by the British connection.

Within the group, these polarities of identity were not quite so pronounced as the discussion might suggest.   John and Fred acknowledged the critical role of Britain in founding Canada and credited the British connection with preventing Canada's assimilation by the United States. Jim and Peter mentioned the richness and uniqueness that cultural diversity brought to Canada and were willing to accept that Canada could not be "frozen in time," as Peter noted, in a fundamentally British framework of identity.

The ambiguity the group experienced relative to the role the British connection played in the Canadian identity and the evident differences in perception about even those communal images that had helped to provide national identity with its mythic structure represented what was essentially the beginning of a hermeneutic awareness among the members of the group. In Gadamer's terms this implied an understanding that we are always in "situations" that affect how we think and act and that "The very idea of a situation means that we are not standing outside it" (1975, 269). Rather than remain outside of the question, we now found ourselves situated within it: National identity and individual identity were no longer separate or separable concepts.

This quality of "situatedness" and the ambiguity of such a condition comprise a critical aspect of poststructural action research. Carson describes poststructural action research as the ability "to remain in the space between" (1989, 14), a phrase that recalls Aoki's comments that teaching is "multiplicity growing from the middle" (1992, 19). Additionally, the revelatory nature of this preliminary discussion brought us into Gadamer's hermeneutic circle.   The comparatively open discussion of our views about national identity and our willingness to publicly raise our own biases, especially Fred and John's willingness to share their highly personal accounts, matched Gadamer's description of hermeneutics as the ability to "let what is alienated by the character of the written word or by the character of being distanciated by cultural or historical distances speak again. This is hermeneutics: to let what seems to be far and alienated speak again" (Gadamer in Gallagher 1992, 4).

The willingness to let the alienated "speak again" further linked our discussions both to hermeneutics and to collaborative action research, but it also raised critical issues of power and representation that all qualitative research must address.   In terms of their connection to hermeneutics, our discussions were founded on what Paul Ricoeur (1981) has called the "hermeneutics of trust." This trust is predicated on the assumption that "both partners [in hermeneutic discourse] must have the good will to try to understand one another" (Gadamer in Gallagher 1992, 23).   But collaboration and trust imply more fundamental moral issues, as Carson reminds us; they imply a sense of obligation. For Carson, obligations transcend the abstractions of ethics in that they render relationships personal and immediate: "Obligations call us...For it is to us personally that the obligation is addressed" (1994, 8). Both the sense of trust and good-will that mark Ricoeur and Gadamer's hermeneutics and the personal obligation that Carson has noted characterized our own action research group. And as was the case with our research issue, we could not stand outside the related issues of power and representation that our research methodology inevitably raised. We had become in Sumara and Davis's terms "complicit" in our research in such a way that we had become "folded into the collective character of the settings" in which the research took place (1997, 310).

The issue of representation is a critical question in action research. As John Elliott (1991) has noted, the question of whether action research can produce changes in teaching practice relies upon "dismantling the value structure of privacy, territory and hierarchy and substituting the values of openness, shared critical responsibility and rational autonomy" (1991, 67).

But this dilemma further implies the need for accurate, fair and ethical representation of the activities and discussions of the group. Because this act of representation involves interpretation, particular care must be taken to verify and validate what was said.   As Carson has noted: "Obligations happen" (1994, 8). In a more elliptical way, Fred noted the same kind of considerations.   Talking to Sunita about her sense of Canadian identity, he said: "You know, I've never thought of how being Indian and a woman might give you a different sense of being Canadian...or does it really matter?" It struck me then that both the reflections involved in the question and the uncertain way in which it was put meant that we had developed at least a tentative sense of obligation toward one another.

Closely tied to the issue of representation is the issue of power and in this case particularly the power of modernist identity discourses. It is an issue to which Gadamer does not adequately respond. His discussion of hermeneutics in terms of "letting" the alienated speak again implies a hierarchy of discourse that, ironically, can lead to the invalidation of the voices of those who have been marginalized. Foucault discusses this danger in his essay "Two Lectures":

> Is it not perhaps the case that these fragments of genealogies are no sooner brought to light, that the particular elements of knowledge that one seeks to disinter are no sooner accredited and put into circulation, than they run the risk of re-codification, re-colonization? (1980, 86)

The issue, then, was how to guard against the patronizing tendency to let others speak only so that their voices could be incorporated into Lyotard's "metanarrative of history," or in this case into the "official multiculturalism" that Giroux and Ghosh discuss and that Aoki, Werner, Connors, and Dahlie describe as the tendency to

> look at material details relative to ethnic groups or to romanticize about a heritage more often than to grapple with such issues as pluralism, cross-cultural communication, government policy, language and aboriginal rights, and value conflicts. (1977, 55)

Within the research group, what tended to complicate this dilemma of voice and representation was the equally problematic issue of our research question. What had emerged from the first segment of the action research project was an acknowledgment that national identity was resistant to definition and description. But that very lack of definition meant that one of the critical questions I had laid out for examination in Chapter 1, "How did we as teachers conceive of Canada's national identity?" remained unanswered.

This failure to respond to what was for me a key question was best expressed in Sunita's response to a Canadian Broadcasting Corporation television special on national identity that aired during the course of our initial discussions. We had all agreed to watch the program and to include our reactions to it in our discussions about our perceptions of national identity. The program's host, in searching for Canada's identity,

(Murphy 1997) concluded that we tended to define ourselves in negative terms. That is, Canadians have created an identity through a series of exclusive statements: We are not Americans; we are not British; we are not French.   Sunita returned the next day and reacted to these conclusions in what can only be described as a state of frustrated rage. Her comments pointed to a longing I think we all felt, but had not expressed while at the same time emphasizing the ambiguity classroom teachers experience when teaching the "Canadian Identity" section of the social studies curriculum.

> Why can't we just say who we are? How can not being something be the basis for a national identity? What am I supposed to tell my students? You aren't American and you aren't British and you aren't French, so you must be Canadian? (Sunita)

The entire group shared the frustration Sunita felt.   Despite the evidence of widely divergent understandings of national identity that had emerged in our discussions, there remained a longing for the kind of imagined community that Benedict Anderson describes. The romantic fantasy of unity and communion that characterizes the modernist idea of nation was not easy to abandon. For Zizek (1996), unitary fantasies of national identity represent nothing less that an extension of the libidinal desire of individuals for completion and a return to a kind of maternal plenitude from which they have been excluded.   This desire is particularly observable in nations with colonial pasts or with significant internal divisions (Huyssen 1995).   In such nations, identity is always contextualized by the colonial past and qualified by existing political realities. For example, literary theorist Laura Mulvey concludes that national identity in Canada had always been, at least partly, "a point of resistance, defining the border fortifications against exterior colonial penetration" (1996, 10). And Sarah Corse observes that the central tension between the French and English founding traditions has made the construction of a unitary identity problematic" (Corse 1997, 111). Charles Taylor, mirroring Hobsbawm and Ranger's conclusions about the role of elites in the construction of national identity, further indicates the problematic nature of such constructed identities when they are not publicly accepted:

> Various political arrangements have been negotiated, and something like common understanding of what these involve has existed among those

political elites who negotiated them, but no common formula has ever been accepted across Canada by the population at large. (1993, 102)

Because it is characterized by the lack of a fully realized sense of self, the quest for Canadian identity continues to be expressed in fairly compelling terms. But despite evident longing for a national identity that could be at once "a form of belonging and [an] anchoring of oneself" (Huyssen 1995, 82) and that was clearly given further urgency by the difficult conditions under which Canadians continue the attempt to establish an enduring sense of nation, we had to admit that the notion of "identity through negation" had merit. In the course of our discussion of the documentary, John had voiced this sentiment with the comment: "Well, we've been trying to define ourselves since Confederation. Maybe there is no clear definition, but we're still here; that has to say something about wanting to stay together."

However, it was equally clear that the source of both Sunita's frustration and John's trenchant observation was the ambiguity and tension that classroom teachers live with in their attempt to deal with a curriculum still predicated on modernist concepts of national identity. I think this explains the group's nostalgic longing for shared symbols of national identity and their frustration with the inability of those same symbols to confer an enduring sense of community. Because the Alberta *Program of Studies* continues to attempt to define and construct a national identity at a time when the "'imagined' and 'constructed' aspects of allegedly 'natural' nationhood are both more visible and more problematic" (Corse, 1997, 112), it is unlikely that teachers' sense of longing and frustration will diminish.

At the conclusion of this first stage of the action research project I was very uneasy. In a sense, I felt that we remained in a state of stasis that had been characteristic of the early stages of the action research project I describe in Chapter 3. Had we moved past Megill's absurdist dilemma? Did we remain trapped in a "state of tension with the given?" Neither my original question about teachers' perceptions of national identity nor the related but more practical question of how to teach the concept in more relevant and imaginative ways had been dealt with. As we moved into the next stage of the project, an examination of the way national identity was treated in the curriculum, I found myself increasingly concerned that the end-point of our discussions would continue to be frustration and uncertainty rather than movement toward a positive change in our teaching practice.

Part II: Exploring the State of the Given

> Perhaps [ethnocultural diversity is] not as, what's the word, visible. It's not as much of an issue yet but in places like Toronto, Vancouver, especially Victoria it is an issue....It's not a matter of what you would like, it's there already. (Anne, a student teacher)

Anne's comment is a revealing observation about the dilemma she feels when facing the prospect of teaching in ethnically diverse classrooms. On the one hand, it is an acknowledgment of the changing demographics of Canadian society and of the classroom environment. On the other, it is difficult to deny the anxiety and incipient hostility such an acknowledgment betrays. Faced with the "other" becoming, in Anne's words, both "visible" and an "issue," she raises, by implication, the question of how national identity is presented in the curriculum and how teachers react to that presentation.

As social studies teachers, the curriculum frames the world in which we work. But that same world is also a place of constant human interactions, the place where relationships *insist* in a way that eludes models of teaching predicated on knowledge transmission. As such, the lived experience of the classroom frequently dictates the pedagogical agenda at least as much as the strictures of the curriculum (Aoki 1988). In situating themselves between these two realities, teachers inevitably find themselves in the position of mediators. However, mediation does not imply neutrality. Teachers cannot adopt a kind of ironic Cartesian detachment that sees the curriculum as one pole, their students as another, and the function of education as nothing more than the construction of appropriate links between the two. To do so is to empty teaching of its moral content and, more important, it is to absolve oneself of the personal obligation implied in the varying teacher-student relationships that emerge in classroom contexts.

In terms of how national identity is portrayed in the Alberta *Program of Studies*, these observations have particular significance. Rapid changes in the ethnocultural composition of the province have been reflected in Alberta's classrooms. These changes have brought with them changing perceptions of Canadian identity, which further imply changing roles for teachers as they deal with the concept of national identity. Furthermore, the close relationship between teachers' individual identities and their understandings of national identity that has already been noted has implications for how teachers view the curriculum and how they integrate the "official" portrayal of national identity into the classroom setting.

As we moved on to examine how Canadian identity was represented in the *Program of Studies*, Anne's concerns increasingly came to mind. It quickly became clear that, like her, the group experienced a significant degree of ambivalence about the implications increasing pluralism held for Canadian identity. Our discussions highlighted the tensions that existed between the curricular portrayal of national identity and how classroom teachers perceived and taught the concept.

The identity theme of the *Program of Studies* has already been examined in Chapter 4, but in our group the focus was slightly different. As classroom teachers, we were concerned with the way national identity was defined and how we reacted to that definition.

From this perspective, it is useful to revisit those aspects of the definition of national identity that most engaged the group. The first was what Fred called "the usual motherhood statement." In simple declaratory terms it was asserted that "Canadians identify with community, region and nation" (Government of Alberta 1990, 13). The second proved much more contentious within the group because of its prescriptive nature. The phrase "bilingualism and multiculturalism are fundamental to the Canadian identity" was discussed in terms that revealed that ethnicity and regional identification were very much at odds with the finality implied by the statement (Government of Alberta 1990, 14).

By this stage of the project, we had already reached a tentative consensus about the absence of a clearly defined Canadian national identity, and although the attempt at definition by exclusion had been grudgingly accepted, it was not particularly comforting. Something of this uncomfortable Lacanian binary that paired lack with desire is captured in Allen Smith's blunt conclusion that in terms of a viable Canadian identity, "not only do Canadians lack what is necessary to put together a totalizing idea of the classically nationalist sort so clearly evident in the United States; they have not even been able to cobble something together from what they do possess" (1994, 10). In the face of the acknowledged lack of Smith's "totalizing idea," the absolute certainty underlying the statement that bilingualism and multiculturalism were "fundamental" to Canada's identity was the source of much dispute within the group.

Unpacking an Official Identity

In some senses, this dispute resolved itself into a discussion about two quite different tropes of Canadian identity.   One represented an unrealized modernist past and the other an uncertain and ambiguous postmodern future.

In terms of the unrealized past, Sunita expressed the view that from her perspective Canada was clearly not a bilingual nation in any more than official terms:

> Who speaks French? My kids went through immersion, and they don't speak French. It would make more economic sense if they learned Mandarin or Japanese or Spanish. Besides, after we teach the fur trade and the Riel Rebellion, there's not much else until you get to Quebec and what's happening today and frankly, my students just aren't that interested anymore. (Sunita)

Even though Sunita's opinions represented what amounted to a direct attack on the curricular "canon" of Canadian identity, her comments were supported by most of the group. What surfaced constantly in our exchanges was the perception that bilingualism was a political issue more related to federal power struggles than it was a defining point of national identity. Jim, pointing out the role of Quebec in the success of the federal Conservative and Liberal parties, noted that "we all know that Trudeau set up bilingualism as a way to keep the political support of Quebec, and federal governments since then have continued the policy." John introduced a new dimension to our discussions when he raised questions about the legitimacy of bilingualism based on regional differences. "Bilingualism," he noted, was "fine for Ontario and New Brunswick where there is a large French population," but the French Canadian influence in the West was so limited that "for us [western Canadians] there's no real reason to focus on it."

In one sense, these sentiments revealed teacher concerns about the relevance of bilingualism to the Alberta *Program of Studies*. But in another sense, they pointed to the failure to generate a sustainable national myth around the concept of bilingualism. It is important to recall the general consensus among historians of nationalism that nationalism is a *constructed* rather than naturally occurring phenomenon. As Ernest Gellner has noted: "Nationalism is not the awakening of nations to self-consciousness: it *invents* [my italics] nations where they do not exist (1994, 169). And as has already been noted, education systems in all countries are a critical functional aspect of that invention. But the question then emerges: What if the process of invention fails? In our discussions, it was quite clear that among the members of the group bilingualism had not become, in Renata Salecl's terms, part of the "fantasy structure" of the nation.

Analogous to Benedict Anderson's (1995) concept of the nation as a form of "communion," the idea that individuals must somehow participate in the "fantasy" of the nation implies the construction of appropriate myths, images, or symbols that will somehow "call out" to the people of the nation in terms they can respond to and in which they can recognize themselves.[1]

The difficulty of manufacturing and sustaining national fantasies at a time when the concept of the nation state itself is under question has already been noted. This dilemma is made even more problematic when the fantasy structure of the nation itself is weak. As Canadian political theorist and philosopher Will Kymlicka has remarked, "We do not have the sort of mythic history that other countries do" (1992, 37). In terms of the construction of national identity, the implications this lack has for Canadian education are significant. On the one hand, from a purely modernist perspective, it suggests the need for concerted efforts to create and maintain a viable set of national myths for our students. However, the very fact of the concern expressed by Kymlicka and others (Granatstein, Taylor, and Hodgetts) represents undeniable evidence of the difficulty of such a task. Acknowledgment of the problematic nature of constructing a sustainable sense of national identity betrays itself in the ambiguity contained in Kymlicka's discussion of the role the education system should play in the construction of national identity. In highly qualified terms he writes, "If shared national identity is essential, and if identity flows as much from a sense of history as from shared values, then we need to find a form of citizenship education that will enable Canadians to find a sense of pride and shared identity in our history" (1992, 47).

But the unstated question is whether such a mutual discovery is possible given the deficiencies in the mythic structure of Canadian identity he mentions earlier. This tentative questing for the foundations of a renewed national identity is very much evident in the writing of Jeremy Webber. In *Reimagining Canada: Language, Culture, Community, and the Canadian Constitution,* Webber notes that "the soul of our identity as Canadians is the conversation we have had in this rich and magnificent land" (1994, 319). For all its sonority, however, there is little that is substantial in the statement beyond the underlying hopefulness of its tone.

This qualified support for the development of national identity is very far from Vincent Massey's notion of the making of the Good Canadian, but it is characteristic of the problematization of the idea of national identity in recent years. Alan Cairns, for example, notes the regionally based "fragmentation" of national identity that raises fundamental questions about the legitimacy of such national myths as the "two founding nations." He concludes that to live outside central Canada is "to catch a glimpse of the Canadian future in which duality, founding peoples, the Plains of Abraham, British constitutional traditions and the cleavages of federalism have diminished credibility" (1993, 9). But in Alberta, the curriculum had specifically and clearly established bilingualism as one of the pillars of Canadian identity, yet its legitimacy was questioned in terms that implied that most group members felt, as did Alan Cairns, that the concept had "diminished credibility."

In a broader sense, this questioning of bilingualism represented the kind of tension we felt between the modernist dictates of the curriculum and our emerging, more fluid, perceptions of national identity. What occupied the space between the two perceptions was a question that resolved itself into an ambiguous tautology: If not bilingualism, then what? If we accepted the inherent truth of Joan Scott's assertion that identity is "an ongoing process of differentiation, relentless in its repetition, but...subject to redefinition, resistance and change" (1995, 11), then we could not "fix" national identity around specific and immutable points of identification. But did such an acceptance invalidate any attempt to investigate national identity? In response to this concern, it emerged that our discussion of the second "fundamental" aspect of Canadian identity offered possibilities for a focused, yet more flexible, examination of national identity.

Identity as Ambiguity

If the trope of bilingualism held little validity as a defining characteristic of national identity, multiculturalism certainly did. Within the group, Fred, John, and Sunita had each discussed their understanding of national identity through the lens of their own ethnicity. Even those group members whose ethnic background made them part of the dominant society had acknowledged the "truth" of the plural nature of Canadian society. But the trope of pluralism had ambiguous meanings for most of the group members, and how pluralism was conceived and discussed within the group tended to reveal deep divisions about both the form Canadian identity should take and the role the curriculum should play in the construction of identity.

Broadly, two specific "camps" emerged. Some supported the idea, in Shehla Burney's terms, of "official multiculturalism" which boils [the concept down] to curry, perogies and Caravans-excluding 'others' from the mainstream of discourse where actual power resides" (Burney, in Grant and Sachs 1995, 132). Speaking of this kind of pluralism, Peter noted that the demographics of Canadian society were changing and that this change needed to be reflected in the curriculum:

> Different cultural groups should be allowed to celebrate their cultures. I take my kids to Heritage Days every year, I think it's important, but at the same time we have to expect that they [immigrant groups] will adapt to Canadian culture. If we don't, I think there is a risk of a kind of Balkanization of Canada where we won't have any common identity at all. (Peter)

For Peter, and for those who supported his understanding of pluralism, the representation of multiculturalism currently sanctioned by the Alberta social studies curriculum That asks the question: "How are bilingualism and multiculturalism strengthening Canada?" (Government of Alberta 1990, 9) set the appropriate tone. Pluralism was to strengthen Canada through the contributions it could bring to the cultural capital of the nation. From the perspective of schooling, such a perspective, meant as Jim said, "studying the different groups that make up Canada and emphasizing the positive contributions they have made to Canadian society."

Viewed in these terms, Canadian identity was best represented in geologic terms as a series of accretions to which each successive wave of immigration contributed a new layer. Any irregularities (conflicts, racism, and violence) would inevitably be smoothed over in time. In many ways it was a hopeful vision of the future of Canadian identity, and it provided schools with productive and positive roles to play in the construction of the "geography" of Canadian identity. Without realizing it, Jim, Peter, and John were conforming to the assimilationist role schools and curriculum have played in the past. Such an understanding of pluralism certainly has currency among those who are earnestly attempting to redraw or reimagine Canadian identity for the twenty-first century. Jeremy Webber, for example, speaking of multiculturalism has noted that "multicultural communities do not want linguistically-based political autonomy. Their *ethic* [my Italics] is one of participation in the broader society, of involvement, of contribution" (1994, 217).

But this relatively unproblematic conception has been as challenged in scholarly circles as it was within our group. John Mallea, for example, concludes, in direct opposition to Jeremy Webber, that some kind of linguistic autonomy is critical to many multicultural groups, and that furthermore, "the language of instruction reinforces the more general role of language-one of the most effective mediators of relationships between groups-in helping reproduce dominance and subordination among Canada's racial and ethnocultural groups" (1989, 48).

In her investigation of the closure of a multicultural school in Ontario, Bonny Norton Pierce cites the poignant comments of "Maria," an Italian Canadian student: "A lot of commercials you see are about ethnic people. They show commercials about Canada and different ethnic people. And it's like they're trying to say, 'This is an ethnic country, be proud.' But then you get the people themselves in Canada who just don't look at Canada that way" (1995, 175). Such observations suggest a more problematic and ambivalent understanding of pluralism, both in terms of how it affects Canadian identity and of how it should be presented in schools.

Certainly Jim's description of multiculturalism and of the role of schools in teaching the concept did not go unchallenged within the group. And the terms in which the "contributions" approach was challenged left little doubt that there were deep divisions within the group over the issue. Fred was the first to raise objections:

> But how do you know each group wants to "contribute," and besides, who decides what a "positive" contribution is? My parents were loyal, hard-working Canadians all their lives, but they still got called Nazis in the Second World War. That's not something you can easily forget. (Fred)

Sunita voiced her concerns in similar terms but added a more contemporary focus:

> I am proud of what Indians have contributed to Canada. But it's one thing to get dressed up and go to the Indian Pavilion at Heritage Days; it's something totally different if my kids get called "Pakis" the next day. (Sunita)

And in reference to the role of education in teaching about multiculturalism, both Fred and Sunita were adamant that some idea of the conflicts—both past and present—inherent in cultural relations within plural societies was critical. From their perspective, the curriculum needed to include representations of the differences between cultures and of how these differences played themselves out over time.

Because of the differing perceptions of ethnicity and identity that had already emerged within the group, it was hardly surprising that there were differences about the meaning of multiculturalism and about the position the curriculum should take on the issue. What was of more interest to me was the terms both sides used to express their views.

Jim, Peter, and John reflected what could only be called the modernist paradigm. For them, a strong identity was a critical aspect of the nation state, and the state itself had a vital role to play in preserving and sustaining that identity. They were proposing a metanarrative of national identity that supposed some set of universal symbols that framed the discourse of nationalism. For them, as for Benedict Anderson, the possibility remained that some kind of common imagining could knit the nation together. Education and, more specifically, the curriculum were to be placed in the service of the state in the production and preservation of a national identity among the youth of the nation. Pluralism, because of the vitality of its "positive" contributions to the nation, could be used to strengthen the state. And education could further aid in this contribution by highlighting the additions to the nation's cultural capital made by various immigrant groups.

Fred and Sunita saw things differently. In the emphasis they laid on the personal and the local in terms of their understanding of pluralism and in their acceptance of difference as an aspect of multiculturalism, they established what Henry Giroux has called a border pedagogy of resistance.   The terms of this resistance rejected the modernist concept of national identity as metanarrative, while it introduced the notion of a previously marginalized "other" into any discussion of national identity. An "other" that Michael Peters has noted has typically been excluded from liberal nationalist discourse when it "does not or cannot exhibit the universal characteristics of the formal idea" (1995, 45). From Fred and Sunita's perspective, their "otherness" was reflected in their view that education should not necessarily function as an arm of the state in the construction of national identity and that pluralism itself was more productively taught as a difficult process involving both conflict and accommodation.

Factional Disputes, Othering, Fragmentation

Within the group I found myself siding with Fred and Sunita. Like them, I was less and less willing to accept the uniformity implied by a construct of national identity predicated on modernist principles. Through our discussions I had come to see national identity in much more problematic terms, terms that suggested that the curriculum could be as much an impediment to an understanding of national identity as it was an instrument of its creation. However, this subject position carried with it critical implications for both the hermeneutic discourse we had been engaged in and for the sense of mutual obligation basic to our own project and to all action research.

As a member of a faction within the group, I feared my role in the hermeneutic circle was seriously compromised. As one who in Gadamer's description, "does not just repeat what he has been told in advance or dictated; [but rather] speaks for [the other] (Gadamer in Michelfelder 1989, 51), there was inevitably an aspect of interpretation in my account of our deliberations, but the question of representation in such a polarized environment remained. Was I speaking with a genuine sense of obligation toward all the members of the group? In both Caputo's and Carson's terms, such an obligation was both immediate and personal and transcended the ethical, if neutral, imperative to render our discussions accurately and in as objective a form as possible (Caputo 1993; Carson 1994). And, moreover, as the division grew over the meaning and importance of multiculturalism and over how it should be taught in school grew, I found myself concerned not simply with maintaining the integrity of the process of hermeneutic discourse and action research but about the future of the project itself.

Division and tension increasingly characterized our discussions over questions of national identity, the curriculum, and the role education should play in building a national identity. And the division itself was not easily or conveniently drawn along ethnic lines. John, while conscious of his own ethnic heritage and of the difficulties his family had faced because of the hostility of the host society to his "otherness," still believed, as did Peter and Jim, that unifying symbols were critical to the formation of national identity and that the role of the school system should be the cultivation of the awareness and legitimacy of such symbols among students.

From John's perspective, definitions of contemporary national identity formation that emphasized fluidity and difference as much as commonality and stability were at best pale imitations of what national identity should be and at worst left students with no fixed points of reference on which to ground their identities. His concerns point to the attractions modernist forms of national identity still retain despite their problematization. Thus, even if current symbols of national identification do not (in Ducrot's terms) "call out" to the nation, modernist national identity retains (sometimes even for those that it has marginalized) the romantic and ambiguous *promise* of community. I think it was this promise that held John to the definition of national identity that the curriculum offered.

In theory, the tension and division our discussions generated could be placed within the context of both action research and hermeneutic discourse. Discussing the process of teacher evaluation from an action research perspective, John Elliott refers to the resolution of differences in opinion that emerge in the collaborative process as a series of "negotiated ambiguities" (1991, 94) and later elaborates on the idea with the observation that

> the appropriate context for handling [disagreements] is open and free dialogue in which [the participants] reflect together about their own and each other's interpretations of the facts and the evaluative perspectives embedded in them....Moreover, such dialogue need not result in total agreement. Both [participants] may emerge from it having modified and changed their views. (p. 103)

In the same vein, Carson (1994) has commented on the "näive notion of democracy as equality in Carr and Kemmis" suggesting instead that: "a richer meaning comes from acknowledging that we collaborate because we are different, the tensionality of difference gives collaboration." (Carson, Terry. Conversation with the author, 20 March 1996)

Within hermeneutic circles, the emergence of conflicting viewpoints is more than implied by Gadamer's notion of shared discourse as the attempt (in a process analogous to Elliott's notion of examining the "evaluative perspectives" embedded individual interpretation) "to raise to awareness those prejudices that guide and condition the process of understanding" (1984, 291).

But knowledge that tension and division could be placed within the framework of both hermeneutics and action research did not ease the immediate dilemma of how to go forward in a polarized atmosphere. I found myself thinking back to Anna Jameson's description of politics in Upper Canada in the late 1830s: "There reigns here a hateful factious spirit in political matters" (1972, 99). For what had emerged in the second aspect of the research was exactly the political: Ideological lines had been drawn, positions had been taken, and factions had developed. Clear evidence of this polarization emerged in a debate between Sunita and Jim over the issue of how cultural difference fit into a definition of national identity. Jim accepted that ethnocultural groups had a right to self-expression and acknowledged that this meant the retention and preservation of a variety of cultural attributes. But he drew the line at the extension of such self-expression beyond specific ethnocultural communities.

> I just can't accept that we have to accept things like Sikhs wearing turbans in the RCMP. The Mounties are part of what makes Canada unique. If you let all minorities bring their own cultural beliefs and practices what would happen to the Force? How could it be a symbol to all Canadians when there would be nothing in common, not even a uniform to keep it together? (Jim)

Sunita could not agree. She emphasized that Canada's identity was not tied to a series of fixed and invariable symbols and that to require individual ethnocultural group to "stay within their own boundaries" was both racist and dangerous to the fabric of Canadian society as a whole.

> Look, Canada is nothing but a nation of immigrants. You can't simply say that after your group came all the others that come after have to be like you. If you do those of us who came "too late" become second class citizens. But if you really believe in multiculturalism you have to accept that what is a Canadian will change over time. The RCMP is a historical fact and a symbol for a particular time, but it is also an organization today and it should change with the times. If it doesn't, how can all Canadians feel proud of it? (Sunita)

While this exchange, in itself, was strong evidence of the vitality and relevance of the issue of national identity in the curriculum, the key question at this point became more technical than conceptual: How could we retrieve the goodwill and sense of mutual obligation that was critical to continuing the project in the face of such division?

One hopeful response to this question emerged through our discussion and interpretation of the texts we had chosen for the third segment of the research project. But achieving this response required the formulation and consensual acceptance of a tentative theory of difference with regard to pluralism in Canadian society, and it meant the resignation of one of the members of the research group.

Part III: Interpreting Ambiguity

> It is right for me while walking in the wood to use every experience and every discovery to learn about life, about the past and the future. But since the wood is created for everybody, I must not look there for facts and sentiments which concern only myself. Otherwise....I am not interpreting a text, but rather *using* it. (Eco 1994, 10, author's italics)

Umberto Eco's discussion of the temptations of the interpretative process and, by inference, of its rules of conduct had particular significance for the project as we moved into the third component of our research. At its conclusion it was fair to state that, by and large, we had obeyed Eco's cautionary injunction. But the dangers implied by what Eco terms "moving within the narrative wood as if it were our own private garden" (p. 10) had caused one member to leave the group.

As a group, we had decided to investigate two texts: One presented an alternate vision of Canadian identity, the other suggested new ways to structure the curriculum itself. In terms of redefining Canadian identity, we chose Charles Taylor's essay "Shared and Divergent Values" in his collection of writings, *Reconciling the Solitudes: Essays on Canadian Federalism and Nationalism* (1993). As a work on alternate curriculum design, we decided to examine Patrick Slattery's *Curriculum Development in the Postmodern Era* (1995). Both texts were chosen at my suggestion in response to questions from the group about what represented interesting points of departure in writings both on Canadian identity and in the curriculum field.

My suggestions represented my interests at the time. Taylor's book, a compilation of his writings on identity from 1965 to 1992, is a kind of intellectual history of the attempt of central Canadians to move beyond a conception of Canadian identity predicated on the cultural and linguistic dualism of Trudeau liberalism. I chose Taylor's work in particular because of its ambiguous treatment of identity in a period when even those who remain firmly committed to a mythic structure of national identity based on the equal contributions of "two founding nations" must acknowledge the presence of "other" in Canadian society.

And because postmodern writing tends to emphasize national identity as a process of the enunciation of difference (Scott 1995) and as a series of boundary transgressions in which the "other" confronts the dominant society with the fact of its existence, and of the unavoidable relation between the two (Bhabha 1995), I chose Slattery's text. In his attempt to define what a curriculum of postmodernism might look like, Slattery established a model that I felt might have some importance in our attempt to reimagine the national identity section of the *Program of Studies*.

Deep Diversity and Deeper Division

We began with Taylor's essay in which he introduces a concept of pluralism that he describes as "deep diversity" (1993, 183). For Taylor, "deep diversity" is the only acceptable response to national identity formation in the wake of the rejection of the idea of a "two-language federation" that was at the heart of the failed Meech Lake Accord (p. 182).

Briefly, "deep diversity" moves beyond simple acknowledgment that "there are great differences in culture and outlook and background in a population that nevertheless shares the same idea of what it is to belong to Canada" (p. 182). Such a view remains the state-sanctioned vision of multiculturalism and is best encapsulated in the federal government's recent assertion that

> Multiculturalism is a fundamental characteristic of Canadian society. Since 1971, the federal Multiculturalism Policy has contributed to a vision of Canadian society based upon such Canadian values as equality and mutual respect regardless of race, ethnicity, language or religion (Canadian Heritage 2000, 1)

and further, that in terms of the realization of a common national identity, Canada encourages [all Canadians] to integrate into their society and take an active part in its social, cultural, economic and political affairs (ibid.)

The sense of common values, state involvement in national identity formation and "common imagining" of the nation on the part of its citizens implicit in the document suggests the strongly modernist "first level" understanding of diversity that Taylor dismisses as thoroughly inadequate (1993, 181). Instead, in his essay he urges that Canada move to a "second level" or "deep diversity" as a more viable expression of national identity. Such a conception suggests that

a plurality of ways of belonging would also be acknowledged and accepted. Someone of, say, Italian extraction in Toronto or Ukrainian extraction in Edmonton might indeed feel Canadian as a bearer of individual rights in a multicultural mosaic....But this person might nevertheless accept that a Québecois or a Cree or a Dene might belong in a very different way, that these persons were Canadian through being members of their national communities. (1993, 183)

And while Taylor acknowledges that such a diffusion of the more traditional structures of national identity may violate the Western (and modernist) vision of the liberal state, he concludes that the "only way" states such as Canada can survive is by adopting the "pluralist mould" (p. 184).

In many ways, Taylor's response to the death of the idea of a nation unified by bilingualism mirrors E. B. Hodgetts's earlier conclusion that any attempt to formulate a unified national identity was "both futile and undesirable...in a vast, multi-ethnic country like Canada" (1968, 119). For both, the solution was to move beyond modernist conceptions of national identity that remain bound to a particular time and space and predicated on the prior existence and mythification of what Jules Michelet called *le peuple* (Michelet 1973). Instead, Hodgetts and Taylor present national identity in terms of a theory of difference that suggests that national identity is contingent and contextual and is a function of how Canadians respond to the issues of difference and accommodation in a multicultural society.

Thus, for Hodgetts, despite "the almost limitless diversity of our open, pluralistic society," Canada was still unique "because of the particular set of problems its people face at any given time," and therefore, "the extent to which Canadians are aware of their identity depends on the depth of their understanding of these problems" (1968, 119–20). And for Charles Taylor, "in many ways accommodating difference is what Canada is all about" (1993, 181).

Taylor's arguments have found favor with such scholars as Michael Ignatieff (2000) and Will Kymlicka (1989; 1995). Both have supported Taylor's contention that in multinational states it is critical to recognize and accept ethnocultural difference. Writing about the various threats to the fabric of civic society in plural cultures, Kymlicka notes that if the "cultural structures" of minority communities are damaged or eliminated, these communities will not be able to make informed decisions about what constitutes the good life within society (1989, 165). More recently Kymlicka has proposed that plural states (and particularly Canada) adopt what he terms "multicultural citizenship" a model structured around the idea that "members of a polyethnic and multinational state must not only respect diversity, but respect a diversity of approaches to diversity" (1995, 190). Michael Ignatieff has expressed support for much the same approach. Speaking of national identity construction in Canada, he notes:

> To commit ourselves to the idea that the search for national unity has no end is not to despair; but merely to acknowledge that it is the very essence of nation-states that they harbor within them incompatible visions of the national story. Holding a nation together does not require us to force these incompatible stories into one, but simply to keep them in dialogue with each other and, if possible learning from each other. (2000, 136)

But ironically, given their liberal origins, such plural and fluid conceptions of national identity speak directly to postmodern formulations of nationalism. On the one hand, they problematize the unique and autonomous national identity that modernism presupposes as the basis for the nation, and on the other, they present the nation itself as an ongoing series of negotiated differences in which the previously marginalized "other" emerges to confront the dominant society with the problematic fact of its difference. Writing of Canada in particular, Linda Hutcheon has observed that this postmodern sense of marginality may well be a critical aspect of our national identity "since the periphery or the margin might also describe Canada's position in international terms, perhaps the postmodern eccentric is very much a part of the identity of the nation" (1988, 3).

Although it is quite clear that Taylor, Kymlicka, and Ignatieff would not categorize themselves as advocates of postmodernism, they do raise questions and propose solutions that present national identity in a much more open and ambiguous light than do modernist scholars such as Benedict Anderson.[2] Within our group, this openness and ambiguity stimulated a debate that prompted us to formulate our own theory of difference. But in the process of formulating this theory, the factionalism that had gradually emerged in the earlier stages of the project broke out into open division.

Most of the discussion within the group focused on our interpretation of exactly what Taylor meant by "deep diversity" and what such a concept implied for teaching Canadian identity. Jim, in particular, had serious reservations. "If being a Canadian means completely different things to each of us," he noted,

> how could we possibly have a national identity? What would you teach in class? That we can all make [national identity] up as we go along? What does that leave our kids to believe in? [Taylor's concept] has nothing definite to give students [but] a sense of who they are, and it ignores our history and the role the English and French had in building this country. If you're going to use [deep diversity] to teach national identity, you might as well just give the whole idea up. (Jim)

For Jim, the definition of pluralism had obviously been stretched beyond acceptable bounds. His unwillingness to entertain a concept of diversity that moved beyond "official multiculturalism" was abundantly clear, as was his understanding of national identity in essentially unambiguous (and modernist) terms. From Jim's perspective, the identity of the nation continued to remain grounded around the myth of the two founding peoples, while the role of education was to socialize young people into an acceptance of this mythic structure.

A Tentative Theory of Difference Emerges

For the rest of the group, Taylor's suggestion that national identity be based on the acknowledgment of our mutual differences was a source of concern and much discussion. Since the beginning of the project, the idea of an unambiguous national identity grounded around specific (and universally understood) symbols had gradually been discarded. The evidence of our own widely diverging perceptions of such mythic touchstones as the Centennial had brought us to this conclusion. But this verdict, while allowing us to discard modernist conceptions of national identity, posed the same kind of dilemma that was evident in Taylor's writing. If the nation presents itself in ambiguous terms as a set of constantly changing relations bound around difference, what does it hold in common? Is the only acceptable response to pluralism the celebration of what even Taylor acknowledges as the incommensurability of difference?

Jim could not accept such a diffusion of national identity. And although we could see deep diversity as emerging logically from the acceptance of difference as a product of pluralism, the intellectual purity of the idea was of little comfort to some group members. Even while Peter reluctantly accepted that "we seem to think of ourselves as Canadian in different ways," at the same time he expressed concerns over "the balkanization" of national identity that he saw as implicit in the acceptance of deep diversity, and John feared what he termed the "creation of a bunch of ethnic ghettoes." But if Peter and John saw acceptance of difference as a potentially divisive force, Sunita and Fred found a source of hope in Taylor's ideas.

Both expressed the view that deep diversity was not only a logical extension of multiculturalism, but also a vehicle for building a new sense of national identity based on tolerance, understanding and acceptance. In discussing his reasons for viewing deep diversity with optimism rather than with suspicion, Fred developed what became a theory of difference that the group could accept as a basis for reimagining national identity. "We're all different,"

> I think we can see that, but I also think we now understand it too. I don't think we'll ever find the "one thing" that brings us all together, but what it [deep diversity] does give us is a way to be different and accept that others are different too. Nobody here thinks we can be like the US or Britain, but we can develop a sense of mutual tolerance that is a kind of link between us. We can't go back to two nations or three if you count aboriginal Canadians. So it seems to me that the only way for us to stay together is to accept that we will all have different views of what it is to be Canadian. And this means that we have to start discussing our differences in the classrooms. (Fred)

Sunita seized on this conception of national identity in terms that reflected her own ethnicity but that also raised the relevance of deep diversity to the changing nature of social studies classrooms.

> Everyone can see I'm not a WASP, but I am still a Canadian. Maybe if we all understood how each of us sees Canada through different eyes, we'd be

> more tolerant of each other and of the kids we see in classes these days. Ask them about Canadian identity and you'll get as many different responses as there are kids. I just don't think we can tell them there is one right way to be a Canadian. And if they're all going to believe different things about what being Canadian is, we'd better make sure they can accept that others will see things differently. (Sunita)

National identity, then, could best be approached through the idea of difference. Through first examining how we were different, a process that involved examining our own identities and how these individual or group identities related to the identities of others, it might be possible to create a sense of commonality grounded on acceptance of difference. Included in such a conception was the notion that the nation was composed of shifting identities tied to race, religion, culture, region, and gender. Moreover, it was possible that multiple and overlapping identities would emerge. But within what would clearly emerge as a "community of communities" (Weeks in Grant and Sachs 1995, 56), the idea of commonality remained. This commonality is at the very basis of identity formation and is founded on the idea that identity is relational. Thus for Stuart Hall (1991): "The critical thing about identity is that it is partly a relationship between you and the Other. Only when there is the Other can you know who you are" (1991, 15–16).

In their attempt to formulate a theory of difference that could prove broad enough to encompass the difference inherent in the increasingly plural nature of Canadian society, but that could also form the basis for a new pedagogy of national identity, both Fred and Sunita unconsciously mirrored the conclusions of Ghosh and Ray that

> the multicultural reality [of Canada] is significant for schools because they are responsible for preparing all students to participate fully in the multicultural social, political, and economic order while the teachers essentially interact within multicultural classrooms. (1987, 304)

This understanding of the importance of difference and of the problematic dynamics of national identity formation in plural cultures points to the critical role education plays in that process and has significant implications for curriculum design. Speaking of these implications, Diane Hoffman warns that when curricula examine diversity simply as part of the perceived need to "do multiculturalism" as part of an inclusive (and assimilatory) ideology, "culture and identity lose their educative value" (1996, 565). As Aoki, Werner, Connors, and

Dahlie warned much earlier: "For those curricula which do not emphasize multiculturalism as an ever-shifting pattern of values and life-styles, the implication for students is that culture is static and timeless" (1977, 37).

But we had already accepted that culture was not static and timeless and that to continue to assume so meant that students and teachers would have difficulty finding themselves in the curriculum. The issue then was to attempt to find ways of incorporating our understandings of national identity formation into the curriculum in terms that helped create a "just, dynamic, and ultimately viable society" (Mallea, 1989, 123).

Acceptance of the role of curriculum in establishing a dynamic model of national identity formulated on the twin principles of change and the enunciation of difference certainly interested most of the members of the group, but not Jim. His vision of a national identity that was at once stable and universal did not fit with the theory of difference that we had evolved. His concerns over the implications this theory held for education in general, particularly his insistence that it would ultimately inhibit students' ability to develop a sense of national identity, caused him to withdraw from the group.

His departure saddened the group; Jim was a colleague and had been as genuinely committed to the project as anyone. And the sense of mutual obligation that had emerged in the course of our discussions had, in Caputo's terms, forged "the links of 'you' and 'I' and 'we' and 'he' and 'she' that transcended formalist ethical responsibility" (1993, 246).

But in terms of our research, it was a reminder that collaboration involved the mediation of difference and that such mediation could not always be successful. In discussing the implementation of educational change, Michael Fullan raises an issue that helped place Jim's decision in a broader context. He notes that "conflict and disagreement are not only inevitable but fundamental to successful change. Since any group of people possess multiple realities, any collective change attempt will necessarily involve conflict" (1991, 106). But Jim's departure also marked a critical point in the action research project. When he left, we were on the verge of investigating Patrick Slattery's text: *Curriculum Development in the Postmodern Era* (1995). In his absence, and perhaps in some ways because his leaving made us work harder to make the project a success, we developed a stronger sense of purpose. Slattery's structured approach to designing a postmodern curriculum allowed us to begin the process of reimagining what a curriculum of identity founded on difference might look like.

Investigating a Postmodern Curriculum

Writing in *A Postmodern Perspective on Curriculum,* William Doll makes the point that postmodern curriculum represents "a transformative vision" of education and that it is rooted in "richness, recursion, relations and rigor" (1993, 174). This same emphasis on the emancipatory potential of postmodernism is found in Patrick Slattery's work. For him, it is no less than "an emerging concept of utopia" that represents a "vision of hope, justice, compassion, *phronesis*, community, inclusiveness, and dialogue" (1995, 205).

But in terms of how such a vision would play itself out in education, emancipation needs to carry with it a structural framework that suggests in more concrete terms what the thrust of a postmodern curriculum would be. Slattery provides this framework when he notes that "the primary focus [of postmodern education] must remain keenly centered on the particular context of local educational communities and specific cultural concerns as well as individual autobiographies" (p. 251). In his emphasis on the local and the individual contexts of education, Slattery, by extension, rejects the modernist curriculum that traditionally privileges the abstract over the concrete and the general over the local (Beck 1997, 8). Finally, in his acceptance of Richard Rorty's assertion that education needs to "extend our sense of 'we' to people whom we have previously thought of as 'they'" (1992, 192), Slattery underlines the importance of broaching the subject of difference in society.

Within the group, Slattery's vision of postmodern education was received with some skepticism. Teachers, and especially experienced teachers, are well aware of the constraints that govern them. And these constraints go beyond the issues of political disenfranchisement and intensification that Apple (1998) Walkerdine (1986) and Martin (1999) note. They are present in the sheer complexity of teaching, in full and ironic awareness of this complexity, John received Slattery's utopic statement about his vision of postmodern education with the comment: "Well, it sounds great, but I don't think I'll quote it to my social studies class on Monday." The group was much more interested in the parameters (the local, the individual, and the cultural) that Slattery had sketched out as the terrain of postmodern education, and they were generally in agreement with his conclusion, phrased as two rhetorical questions:

> Is the problem [of interesting students in the curriculum] that educators have not perfected the modern methods? Or is the problem that the modern methods are no longer appropriate in a postmodern era? (1995, 42)

In response to these rhetorical questions, Slattery lays out five characteristics basic to postmodern education. These principles formed the building blocks of the postmodern curriculum of national identity we attempted to create. Each was set forth in a manner that emphasized the fluidity and openness of postmodern approaches to education and that encouraged a continuance of the hermeneutic conversations we had been engaged in up to that point. In many respects, Slattery's curriculum conformed to Donald Schwab's injunction that "curriculum is not an endless series of objectives...[nor is it]...necessarily the same for all students of a given age and standing [but rather it is constructed]...in a back and forth manner between ends and means" (1996, 90–91). Slattery, like· Schwab, emphasizes the importance of both process and autobiography in the attempt to make the curriculum more meaningful.

The five characteristics that describe the shape of Slattery's postmodern curriculum have been discussed in Chapter 2. They represent both suggestions for methodological approaches to postmodern curriculum design and the attributes of such a curriculum. After some discussion, we decided to concentrate our efforts on two key principles that seemed particularly representative of our conversations to that point. The first was Slattery's emphasis on the centrality of individual experience to educational understanding; the second, his belief, based on the work of Pinar and Grumet (1976), that education was a process rather than a prescribed set of discrete outcomes.

**First Principle: The Importance
of the Individual in Approaching the Global**

In discussing this principle, Slattery writes:

> First, a process approach to education is capable of engendering a significant reconceptualization of the nature of schooling globally as well as the experience of education locally because it respects the unique development of the individual and recognizes the interrelationship of all experiences. (1995, 252)

Citing William Pinar and Madeleine Grumet's (1976) work on the importance of autobiography to curriculum design, Slattery concludes that the critical concern is to authenticate the individual experience of students while at the same time encouraging them to "make connections to broader concepts" (1995, 253).

Within the group, the significance of individual experience in identity formation had already been demonstrated in our discussions about the symbolic importance of the Centennial.   This first experience of difference had played an important role in our realization that perceptions of national identity were widely divergent, and it had been an initial step toward our formulation of a vision of national identity based on a theory of difference.   Fred's response to Slattery's linkage of the local to the global was typical of the opinions expressed by all of us:

> I think this makes sense. Most of my students can't really imagine Canada as an abstraction. They tend to focus on what affects them immediately. So if we could begin with the way they look at themselves and gradually expand that outward, maybe they would come to see that we have some things in common. (Fred)

Fred's interpretation of the process of national identity formation stood at opposite ends of the spectrum from modernist versions that tend to see the nation as a construct of the state. Furthermore, the assumption about education's role in that process contained within his interpretation placed teachers in a fundamentally different role from the one they now occupied. Rather than instruct about national identity in terms that portrayed the nation as the "timeless and static" and that introduced a Cartesian binary between the teacher as expert and students as unknowing "others," Fred's description suggests that teachers adopt the more authentic role as *pedagogos*.

In David Smith's terms, this role assumes a hermeneutic act of "engagement in which the teacher shows the way by which it is possible for a young person to understand and enter his or her own tradition as a living stream" (1995, 23). But at the same time, in a hermeneutic sense the teacher cannot stand outside of this relationship. As Dieter Misgeld has noted, a hermeneutic attitude involves a mode of inquiry "that refuses to legitimate any predisposition on the side of those inquiring to exempt *themselves* from what is topical in the inquiry" (1983, 162). The kind of reciprocity of engagement implicit in the hermeneutic circle also echoes the postmodern concern for overcoming the hierarchies of "self and other" built into most institutionalized structures. Clive Beck stresses,

> We must think increasingly in terms of student and teachers "learning together"....This is necessary both so that the values and interests of students are taken into account, and so that the wealth of their everyday experience is made available to fellow students *and to their teachers.* (1997, 8; Beck's emphasis)

The hermeneutic and postmodern emphasis on the legitimacy of individual experience and on the possibility of expanding this experience to broader horizons that marked Slattery's first principle of postmodern curriculum development extended naturally into the second principle that we chose to examine: The notion that the curriculum itself must be viewed as a process (*currere*) rather than as a series of specified, testable and achievable ends.

Second Principle: The Racecourse Rather Than the Race: The Postmodern Curriculum as *Currere*

Again, drawing on the work of Pinar and Grumet (1976), Slattery stresses that the postmodern curriculum must emphasize the notion of *currere*. Implicit in this notion is the idea that "curriculum is a verb, an activity...an inward journey" (1995, 56). In Pinar and Grumet's terms this process was to be accomplished with the aid of specific subject matter, but what was taught was clearly secondary to the individual's journey toward self-awareness:

> They" [in this case the humanities] are precisely areas of study, useful only to the extent to which the individual finds them helpful or in some way pertinent to his journey. It is the journey, i.e. the process of individuation, of psycho-social and moral development that must be our central concern. (1976, 29)

More recently, Pinar has written that the sense of "definitiveness that characterize curriculum is a 'tissue of lies'" that masks the "provisional [and] temporal" relationship of the knower to the known (1992, 100). Through his emphasis on curriculum as a process irrevocably bound to identity formation and given his ongoing deconstruction of the modernist metanarrative of the curriculum in favor of a more contingent understanding, Pinar shares much with Slattery's postmodernism.

Slattery's conclusion that a curriculum of postmodernism must move students along a process "from romance, through precision to generalization" (1995, 255) is closely matched by Pinar and Grumet's (1976) four stages of autobiographical reflection: the regressive, the progressive, the analytical, and the synthetic. This process approach to curriculum is evident in the work of other postmodern educational theorists. Henry Giroux (1991), for example, speaks of the need for students to engage in a process of "coming to voice" that situates their own histories within the histories of the larger society and at the same time provides them with the critical skills required to examine the underlying structures of that society. Oliver and Gershman suggest that learning is a shared process in which "students are allowed, in the presence of their intellectual heritage, to be creative—i.e. to actualize their potential" (1989, 167).

In our group, the idea that the curriculum should be a process rather than a series of predefined ends met with some resistance. But the resistance was not based on a rejection of the idea itself; in fact, John, the group member who expressed the strongest reservations about the process approach, was more than willing to admit that "the curriculum as it stands now is not much more than a long shopping list of objectives." Rather, his resistance emerged out of ambiguity. Like the rest of us, he was uncomfortably aware of the dictates of both the curriculum and of formalized evaluation. And, like us, he also sensed that a student-centered pedagogy that stressed development rather than accomplishment would ultimately be a better approach to the issue of difference in plural classrooms. But the disjunction between the two positions—the one obedient to modernist strictures, the other sensitive to postmodern conditions—created a climate of ambiguity and uncertainty.

> What if I do try to focus on this process approach and I can't finish the course? Will Central Office say "Hey, that's OK, just take another crack at it?" Look, I don't mean to be cynical, but is this process approach practical? I like the idea of using students' experiences, and I think I can work it in. I'm just not sure I can serve two masters. (John)

John's concern was a product of the ambiguous position in which most classroom teachers currently work. Caught in what Aoki (1988) has described as the uncertain space between "the curriculum as plan" and the "curriculum as lived experience," and uncomfortably aware of the dictates of outcomes-based education, teachers are frequently, and in many instances justifiably, hesitant to embark on any significant changes in their teaching practices. John's ambiguity was a metaphor for any teacher considering the adoption of an ex-centric pedagogy in which the linear approach of the curriculum was exchanged for what Schwab has termed "a back-and-forth manner between ends and means" (Schwab 1996, 91). I would argue that such a move represents the shifting and permeable postmodern boundaries between the margins and the center.

But the ambiguity John felt was more than a personal dilemma; we all sensed it. And it was both a caution and a challenge to the entire group. If we were to find a way of incorporating Taylor's concepts and Slattery's methodology into a reconceived curriculum of national identity, the ambiguous position that John had adopted would have to become a productive ambiguity.

The Dangers of "Doing" Multiculturalism

Writing in the *American Educational Research Journal,* Diane Hoffman warns that the existing paradigm in multicultural education that seeks to "do good" to minorities represents an unacceptable binary between a patronizing middle-class self and an underprivileged "other." Instead, she suggests the adoption of an approach she terms "reflexive multiculturalism," an approach grounded on:

> the development of knowledge about different ways of seeing the self-other relationship, including more socio-centric, flexible, and layered visions; and, moreover, an openness to seeing these other ways and values as a potential source of learning rather than as incommensurably different, or, alternatively as a threat to oneself. (1996, 564)

I cite Hoffman's prescription because of its similarity in breadth to Charles Taylor's concept of "deep diversity." In her emphasis on the need to bridge the self-other binary currently typical of most multicultural education, she mirrors Patrick Slattery's injunction that a postmodern curriculum must be grounded on the notion that education is both a democratic and reciprocal process.

Writing from a Canadian perspective, the work of Mallea and Ghosh and Ray contain similar conceptions. Mallea, for example, in criticizing existing research on pluralism in education, notes that "ethnicity has been seen as a categorical reference point rather than a process and ethnic groups have been treated as static systems which constrain the political integration of the nation" (1989, 118). And from Ghosh and Ray's perspective:

> Multicultural education must have a human rights approach wherein opportunities would not be hampered because of cultural, racial/ethnic, or gender differences. The educational system, especially teacher education, needs to be altered to take into account racism and sexism in the classrooms. (1987, 306)

Such transformative visions for education are only possible within a different context: one that takes into account the idea of difference while at the same time pointing out the possibilities of shared senses of community. And in terms of national identity formation it implies an acceptance of Homi Bhabha's ambiguous third space of translation, a space that Peter McLaren asserts "requires that identities—especially cultural identities—be seen as decentered structures that are constituted only in relation to otherness" (1995, 109).

McLaren's comments bring the issue back to the research project and the theory of difference we had formulated within the group. Like McLaren, Bhabha, Hall, and others, we had concluded that identity formation was primarily relational, but that these relationships were fluctuating, highly individual, and dynamic. Using Taylor's concept of "deep diversity" and Slattery's postmodern curricular parameters, we began to construct exercises that represented a collective attempt to reimagine a curriculum of national identity.

Our first concern was with the *Program of Studies* itself. We needed to find a legitimate location for deep diversity within the existing curricula. Because many group members shared John's apprehension about whether we could successfully incorporate both Taylor's concept and Slattery's methodology, curricular legitimacy was of prime importance. As Sunita noted: "This is pretty much out of the norm. To make it work, it has to fit with something in the Canadian identity section [of the grade ten social studies curriculum]."

Although there was some irony in turning to a modernist curriculum to give sanction to postmodernist reinvention of that same curriculum, this concern for institutional validation was additional evidence of the ambiguous position that teachers themselves occupy when attempting to initiate change. As John Elliott notes, teachers involved in action research frequently encounter bureaucratic and technocratic obstacles to their research. But despite these obstacles, he encourages teachers to develop a "reflective counter-culture" (1991, 62) that in many ways mirrors Henry Giroux's (1993a) invitation to teachers to develop a pedagogy of resistance within schools.

With these injunctions in mind, we examined the Canadian identity section of the Alberta curriculum for a site for our reinvention. The essentialist description of national identity as predicated on bilingualism and multiculturalism offered limited possibilities because of its static and statist context. Both concepts were to be examined "by referring to our historical background to understand our official policies" (Government of Alberta 1990, 14). But the final generalization in the section provided us with an effective opening into the curriculum. The statement that "interaction among groups influences one's identity" was matched by the instruction that students were to "examine examples of interaction with others in order to understand how they shape one's cultural identity" (Government of Alberta 1990, 14). This instruction was elaborated on to include an examination of such "Related facts and content" as "legitimacy of self," "majority-minority status," "assimilation, cultural maintenance" [and] "cultural promotion" (ibid.).

Because this section emphasized a process approach to the formation of cultural identity and stressed the importance of the individual in that process, the group felt we could safely locate our project within these curricular parameters as we entered into the fourth part of the action research project: the development of exercises predicated on a postmodern reimagination of national identity.

Part IV: Reimagining National Identity

We began with the issue of the legitimacy of self. But for the group the critical issue was self in context. If the postmodern curriculum was to be viewed in terms of Pinar's *currere*, then it was critical to encourage students to move from "romance, through precision to generalization" (Slattery 1995, 255). We created a two-part activity based on the construction of a "Personal Identity Profile" (see Appendix A). The assignment involved the gathering of data on the students' ethnic and cultural heritage and, at the same time, a description, formulated by each student, of their own attachments. This account included information about their interests, the groups they belonged to or identified with, and (most critically) how they would describe themselves as Canadians.

Once the data collection phase of the assignment was completed, the students were to create a two-part poster in which they showed through pictures, symbols, diagrams, words, and images, both the ethnocultural information and the more personal data they had recorded. The critical aspect of the poster was to see if points of overlap or intersection emerged between the personal and the ethnocultural. Because we were concerned with eliminating, as much as possible, the self-other binary between teachers and students implicit in most modernist classrooms, while students were involved in this ethnographic and individual "archaeology," the instructor was to be engaged in the same process. Once the posters were completed they were to be displayed in the classroom for the general viewing. The exercise was to be brought to a close with a class discussion centering on the question:

"What does it mean to me to be a Canadian?"

We felt that approaching the more general question of national identity through the vehicle of individual identity formation coupled with ethnic and cultural identifications matched the process approach Slattery suggested for a postmodern curriculum. Moreover, the endpoint (unlike in most modernist curricula) was not specified in concrete terms. The possibility existed, for example, that students would not see a relation between their personal identity and their ethnocultural identity. And in terms of individual appreciation of Canadian identity, a variety of responses were accounted for.

The likelihood that different perceptions of self, ethnicity, and identity would emerge in the assignment fit Taylor's injunction that "deep" or "second level diversity" needed to take into account a "plurality of ways of belonging" (1993, 183). However, the dilemma of unproblematized difference bothered some group members. Peter, in particular, was concerned that the assignment had no more definite endpoint than a class discussion.

> How are we going to get the kids to accept difference if we don't wrap the assignment up in a more meaningful way? In my experience, class discussions just kind of dribble away or are dominated by certain kids. Wouldn't it be better to have them write an essay, or why not grade the poster? (Peter)

All of us recognized the dilemma of achieving closure in the relatively unstructured environment of class discussions. But my concern was not really to achieve closure at all. It was to maintain the idea that national identity formation in plural cultures was an ambiguous process, and that it could not, in a modernist sense be "resolved" with anything like the finality implied in the curriculum. To do so was to freeze pluralism into a static model that promoted the idea that multiculturalism was a cultural object; a somehow quantifiable "thing" (D. Aoki 1996) that was external to students and the product of the curriculum.

Sunita supported me in this stance:

> I don't think we can just "teach" multiculturalism. We have to live it, and that means accepting what students think about who they are and what they think of Canada. They might not say what I hope they will about tolerance and diversity, but I think they have to be allowed to express their views. (Sunita)

The democratic and dialogic process that refused (in postmodern terms) to privilege one view over another reflected the spirit of Slattery's first principle of postmodern curriculum formation that encourages a rejection of "hierarchical, authoritarian, patriarchal, and hegemonic ideologies" (1995, 252) in the attempt to legitimate students' experiences.

But other reservations were raised about the process of encouraging students to engage in reflection about identity formation. John wondered aloud whether the exercise would have as much value as we hoped if students had not engaged in this kind of process before: "I'm not sure all of my kids can do this at the grade ten level. And if they can't, will they feel they should make an identity up, or just give us stock answers?" Like Peter's concern over closure, John's apprehensions were valid and represented yet another dilemma. Had we taken into account the possibility that by grade ten students might not have established a unique identity or that they would be able to make direct correlations between their own senses of self and the various communities they belonged to? Diane Hoffman notes this same dilemma when she writes that the belief that all students "possess" an identity in what amounts to material form is based on the assumption that there is basically a one-to-one relation between self and culture characterized by a clear, fixed, commitment to a particular cultural or ethnic identity. In this model, gaps or points of nonconformity, degrees of distance, freedom, or flexibility that do in fact characterize identity in the real and infinitely more complex world of culture as it is lived are absent. (1996, 557)

However, as Fred pointed out, the exploration of personal identity provided for through the creation of an individualized identity profile did allow students the freedom to examine identity as a dynamic, overlapping, multilayered process or to describe it in unique, autonomous, and structured terms.

While reservations were raised about the ends of the activity, we all agreed that it made possible the expression of difference in a way that encouraged students to form generalizations about their identities. And through the process of formulating these generalizations, the further possibility of a shared sense of identity built around appreciation of difference emerged. But it remained fundamentally an open-ended process; if a sense of community emerged, we hoped it would be authentic and not in response to the dictates of the exercise, the aims of the curriculum, or the wishes of the instructor.

The second activity built on the sense of individual and group identity explored in the first activity while it attempted to investigate the limits of students' identity attachments. In some senses, the assignment was an attempt to establish the viable parameters of Benedict Anderson's notion of "imagined communities." Thus, students were asked to make a series of identity webs with self at the center. Progressively, they were to add a series of communities, some quite real, others more imaginary, in an ever-expanding web that represented the links they felt to those communities.

Through a schematic examination of their relationships to world, family, ethnocultural community, friends, nation, school, local community, region, and province (to avoid a simple hierarchical ordering of these relationships, the various referents were intentionally jumbled), it was hoped that students would engage in what Charles Taylor calls "exploring the space of deep diversity" (1993, 183). Such an exploration was similar to what Patrick Slattery describes as "kaleidoscopic community sensibility...[in which] individual pluralism in specific contexts gives strength to the whole edifice of education" (1995, 252).

The webs, once completed, were to be displayed in the classroom where students would view them with an end to answering three questions in written form:

1. How is your web different from the other webs?
2. How is your web similar to the other webs?
3. What explains the similarities and differences you noted?

As a final component of the activity students were to write a short essay on the topic:

Do you believe it is still possible to speak of Canada having a single identity?

The question itself was intentionally framed in ambiguous terms that implied a fixed historical identity, a more dynamic identity in the present, and the validation of multiple ways of identifying with the nation. Incorporated into the topic was the idea of difference and the problematic suggestion, raised by Homi Bhabha, of the "impossible unity of the nation as a symbolic force" (1990b, 306).

This conscious attempt to deconstruct the modernist idea of national identity as it is represented in the curriculum reflected our desire to have students explore some of the ramifications of Taylor's notion of deep diversity. At the same time, both the webbing component of the activity and the essay topic held out the possibility that there could be attachments that went beyond the personal and local, thus following Slattery's injunction that a postmodern curriculum should be "local in character, but global in its impact" (1995, 253).

Most of the group accepted the need to expose students to the ambiguous nature of national identity formation through an examination of the concept of difference, but Peter expressed concerns that the essay topic was too manipulative:

> Aren't we leading the kids to the conclusions we want them to reach? Aren't we saying we want kids to tell us that a single national identity is impossible and that we have to accept that Canada is made up of differing groups who may have very different ideas of what it is to be a Canadian? Is this any better than saying Canada is bilingual and multicultural and we all have to believe in those things or we aren't true Canadians? (Peter)

My response to Peter's questions was a simple "yes" to all his queries. Our research had led us to accept the concept of difference as critical to the formation of identity. None of us would have asserted by this time that plural nations could form viable identities based on modernist visions of a single overarching national identity. More than that, however, Taylor's notion of deep diversity pointed to an understanding of national identity that was at once accepting and dynamic.

But such an understanding does not emerge naturally or immediately; as Jerzy Smolicz has written, plural societies need to develop a broad framework of values that promote "the acceptance of cultural diversity as a shared value by [both] the majority group and society as a whole" (1996, 66). This acceptance further implies the incorporation of the idea of difference central to Bhabha's observation that "national cultures are only constituted in relation to that otherness internal to their own symbol forming activities" (1990a, 210). Within the group we were generally convinced that schools had a critical role in promoting the acceptance of diversity that Smolicz discusses and that Bhabha asserts as a critical aspect of the national identity of all states. Furthermore, the concept of postmodern education as *currere* implied an obligation on the part of the teacher to approach national identity formation in a way that encouraged students to engage in the process of moving from their own individual perceptions to progressively broader insights.

With the preparation of the two activities a good proportion of the action research component of the project was completed, but it still remained for us to present our findings. In action research the democratic spirit of collaboration implies more than the willingness of teacher-researchers to work together to improve their teaching practice; it also implies the sharing of the results of the research in some public forum (Elliott 1991). Altrichter, Posch, and Somekh argue that it is a "primary concern of action research to promote the sharing of knowledge and experiences of the teacher-researchers who engage in it, in order to develop classrooms and schools" (1993, 9).

Meeting Ambiguity and Ambivalence Head-On

The forum we chose for sharing the results of our research and thus bringing the action research project to a close was a session at a system-wide teacher in-service day. The presentation focused on our understanding of the need to reimagine the teaching of Canadian identity and involved a brief presentation of postmodernist approaches to national identity and multicultural education. As an effective (we assumed) completion to the presentation, we intended that those teachers in attendance should draw their own identity webs, which we would then discuss.

What emerged instead was a debate over modernism, national identity, and bilingualism, the terms of which reflected the deep divisions that had emerged in our own action research group. The room divided itself roughly into three opposing camps with us in the middle attempting to mediate the discussion. One camp agreed with us that the modernist "foundations" of Canada's national identity delineated in the curriculum did not reflect the reality of their classrooms. But the locus of their discontent was "official" bilingualism, and the terrain they defended was grounded on expressions of the uniqueness of western Canadian identity. Another camp accepted the curricular version of a nation founded primarily on bilingualism and multiculturalism but rejected our suggestions that deep diversity was the only viable response to pluralism and the only acceptable basis for national identity in the 1990s. The third camp, though somewhat smaller, was composed of immersion teachers for whom the concept of national identity was inextricably tied to bilingualism with only a grudging nod given to multiculturalism. The debate that ensued saw the expression of visions of national identity grounded on linguistic dualism, modernist notions of consensual nationalism, and regional identification. We never managed to have teachers draw their Canadian identity webs; I'm not sure what would have happened had we given them marking pens.

Conclusion: The Presence of an Absence

It was not exactly the conclusion we expected, but in some senses it was a symbolically satisfying end to the project. Charles Taylor wrote as an introduction to the notion of deep diversity that recent debates over constitutional change had been more productive of "mutual suspicion and ill will" than of the accommodation of difference that has been assumed to be typical of Canadian identity (1993, 181). However, much like the tropes of national identity that preceded it, the trope of tolerance and accommodation needs careful scrutiny. As Ghosh and Ray have pointed out: "In the coming years we will be confronted with the question of racial and ethnic rights to equal educational opportunity.

Surveys have shown that Canadian society is becoming more, not less racist" (1987, 307). In the face of resurgent racism, within a climate of "mutual suspicion and ill will" Taylor's notion of a national identity based on deep diversity may be in his words, "the only formula on which a united federal Canada can be rebuilt" (1993, 183).

But whether the good-will that such a formulation implies exists is a moot point. As metaphor, both the action research project and the teacher audience we presented to were representative of the serious cleavages that have emerged in Canadian society. Both displayed an ambiguous association with the idea of national identity itself. In terms of identification—particularist tendencies, whether ethnic, linguistic, or regional—seemed to hold much more power than nationalist sentiment.

This in itself was fairly clear evidence of the failure of myth-making at the national level, but it was further corroborated by our discussions within the action research group. Although we reached consensus about developing a theory of difference using Taylor's ideas and based on Slattery's postmodern methodology, it had become quite clear to me by the end of the project that there was no "common imagining" that knit the group together. I found myself turning more and more to Homi Bhabha's problematic discussion of the nation as a series of multiple narratives and to his conclusion that "it is actually very difficult, even impossible and counterproductive, to try and fit together different forms of culture and pretend that they can easily exist" (1990a 209). This sentiment seemed to mirror Hodgetts's equally blunt conclusion that the search for national unity was both "futile and undesirable" (Hodgetts 1968, 119).

But this same sense of uncertainty about the "national project" represents the opportunity to rethink how we conceive of the nation. I think Charles Taylor sensed this backhanded opportunity even as he wrote with some pessimism about the future of the nation. Furthermore, such an opportunity carries with it anthropological sanction. Thus, the French anthropologist Pierre Clastres noted that "to be able to study a society, it already has to be a little decayed" (Clastres in Lyotard 1993, 90). Certainly the disintegration of the "national dream" represents an opening for the examination and redefinition of who we are.

In our action research group we chose to seize this opportunity in the attempt to reexamine our understanding of national identity and in hopes of making the concept more relevant to our students. In doing so, we had entered the ambiguous terrain of identity formation. And in the process of reflecting on national identity, we found ourselves reexamining our own identities. Out of this re-examination had come a theory of national identity founded on difference but grounded in the hope that acceptance of difference would be a force strong enough to bind the nation together. We had also come to see national identity formation as a dynamic process that students could appreciate only through the medium of individual experience and autobiography.

The hermeneutic conversations we had in the course of the project certainly led us to a greater appreciation of the subject positions each of us spoke from and resulted in a much greater understanding of the context of the debate on national identity. But if we achieved the "fusion of horizons" that Gadamer describes as a central aim of interpretation, it was more tied to greater understanding of each other than it was to the texts we examined. Much more than the curriculum documents and the readings we had chosen, *we* were the text we interpreted. As Gadamer notes: "The person with understanding does not know and judge as one who stands apart and unaffected, but rather as one united by a specific bond with the other; he thinks with the other and undergoes the situation with him" (1975, 288). This relation of understanding to empathy which Couture (1997) identifies as one of the bases of poststructural action research emerged in the sense of obligation we developed throughout the course of the project.

The understanding that teachers occupy an ambiguous location between the curriculum and the realities of the classroom, between their own identities and the formal role they assume as teachers, between themselves and their students, and between their roles as teacher and researcher was strongly reinforced during the course of the project. Although ambiguous, this location is not untenable. It represents the productive site between theory and practice that creates "space for ethical reflection on action and multiple possibilities for reflective practice" (Carson 1992, 14). For Sunita, appreciation that the ambiguous location that teachers occupy can be productive meant the release of a certain amount of tension. Near the end of the project she commented: "I have a better understanding of some of the forces that affect me as a teacher. Some I can control, others I can't, but just knowing this helps put things in perspective some times."

Finally, in terms of national identity, the project made it clear that there was space for the reimagination of national identity within existing curricula and that it was possible to engage students in an investigation of the concept of deep diversity using postmodern methodologies. But the project also revealed the widely differing interpretations of national identity we held. These differences ultimately resulted in one member leaving the group. More than that, however, they led me to the conclusion that despite the consensual curriculum of national identity we had created, this consensus was achieved in what Madeleine Grumet calls the "presence of an absence" (1988, 142). Although the reference was meant to suggest that the text as such had no meaning except in terms of the meaning each reader brought to it, it also represents the dilemma of national identity, particularly Canadian identity.

As each reader brings his or her own meaning to the "text" of national identity it becomes increasingly apparent that there is no "common imagining" and that the Good Canadian cannot be reinvented. I will discuss the ambiguous implications this concept holds for education in the final chapter.

CHAPTER 6

No Common Imagining:
National Identity in an Ambiguous Context

I'm not sure what being a Canadian means. (A student)

Part I: Modernism, Absurdity, and National Identity

I began Chapter 3 with a description of an action research project focusing on teachers' perceptions of nationalism in the post-Cold War period. Through the course of that project I began to see links between action research and absurdity. At the time, Alan Megill's description of absurdity as "a state of tension with the given" (1985, 345) struck me as particularly appropriate to the process of action research, which purposefully situates itself in this location in the attempt to bridge the gap between theory and practice in educational research. But more than that, in our collaborative investigation of the contours of this site, it became increasingly clear that the same description could be applied to the relationship between the modernist assumptions of the curriculum and the changed conditions teachers experience in their classrooms and in their perceptions of the wider world. David G. Smith has described teachers in ironic terms as "keepers of the myth of coherence" (1995, 20). The irony, of course, resides in the absurdist position such a function imposes on teachers.

Required to teach a curriculum whose assumptions and legitimacy they no longer uncritically assume, teachers find themselves trapped between the mythic structure of modernism and the postmodern realities the classroom presents to them. The absurdity of this position lends itself to the deep-seated sense of ambiguity teachers feel toward the curriculum. Its strictures place teachers on the margins of power in educational discourses (Apple 1993, 1998; Giroux 1993a) at the same time that the interaction between the curriculum as colonial power and teachers as colonized other creates a kind of pedagogical third space of hybridization where, in Homi Bhabha's terms, "the meaning of cultural and political authority are negotiated" (1990a, 309).

This ambiguity is nowhere more apparent than with regard to the way nationalism and national identity are presented in the curriculum. For teachers and students alike, modernist curricula have portrayed national identity in static terms that effectively exclude the legitimacy of individual experience. But this experience, I would argue, is critical to forming the kind of attachments that make such abstractions as "national identity" viable. As Gadamer reminds us, the artificial division between self and world that characterizes modernism and suggests that individuals can stand outside of history is false and dangerous:

> We cannot extricate ourselves from [history] in such a way that the past becomes completely objective for us....We are always situated in history....I mean that our consciousness is determined by a real historical process in such a way that we are not free to simply juxtapose ourselves to the past. (Gadamer in Gallagher 1992, 90)

The curriculum that reflects this modernist tendency to foster reliance on abstract principles over the local, the immediate, and the personal (Giddens 1990; Borgmann 1992) certainly reinforces this separation; it assumes allegiance to the idea of nation as its first principle while it downplays the importance of the formation of individual identity.

Such a separation is alienating both in and of itself and in terms of the position it forces teachers to occupy. The ambiguity of this condition is perhaps unavoidable. The curriculum will likely always mandate the examination of concepts, facts, and generalizations in ways that are quantifiable and, for that reason, modernist and restrictive, and it will likely remain the function of teachers to translate these objectives into relevant and realizable activities. But its consequences have been largely responsible for the decontextualized, static, and essentially sterile representation of national identity the social studies curriculum presents.

Part II: The Possibilities of Radical Reconceptualization

In their attempts to deconstruct or reinterpret the dominant narratives of identity and education, both postmodernism and hermeneutics offer more dynamic and democratic approaches to teaching national identity. Furthermore, in their appreciation of the uncertainty and ambiguity that characterize daily life, they are particularly appropriate to the ambiguous "in-betweenness" that is a critical aspect of teaching (T. Aoki 1988).[1]

The hermeneutic concern for interpreting identity within the context of time, space, and community is in direct opposition to the modernist tendency to posit a unique and autonomous self separated from these realities. As Charles Taylor (1989) notes, "Each young person may take up a stance that is authentically his or her own; [but] this stance does not originate just in that person: the very possibility of this is enframed in a social understanding of a greater temporal depth, in fact in a 'tradition'" (1989, 39). Thus, the formation of identity involves situating oneself within a tradition rather than standing outside of it. Education from a hermeneutic perspective reflects this same quality of "situatedness" that conceives of schooling as "a process that happens to the human enterprise" (Gallagher 1992, 179).

Postmodernism, too, reflects on the contingent and relational nature of identity. At once antimodern and ambiguous, this sense of uncertainty lends itself to a conception of identity as an indeterminate and never-secured process in which "the I-as-symbol and the I-as-sign, the articulations of difference—race, history, gender—are never singular, binary or totalizable" (Bhabha 1995, 57).

By extension, national identity is seen in equally indeterminate and ambiguous terms. Chantal Mouffe, for example, notes that the political community is a "surface of inscription of a multiplicity of demands" and that such pluralities of demands dictate that "a fully inclusive community can never be reached" (1995, 36). For Homi Bhabha, the nation is a mythic creation whose "cultural temporality inscribes a more transitional social reality" (1990a, 306).

Postmodern resistance to the tyranny of the metanarrative, whether it be the metanarrative of the individual or the metanarrative of the nation, implies a vision of education that is at once local and global and that encompasses both difference and ambiguity. Aronowitz and Giroux assert that when coupled with the modernist concern for "enlightened subjects,"

> the postmodern emphasis on diversity, contingency, and cultural pluralism, points to educating students for a type of citizenship that does not separate abstract rights from the realm of the everyday, and does not define community as the legitimating and unifying practice of a one-dimensional historical and cultural narrative. (1990, 82)

Taken together, postmodern and hermeneutic approaches to education and identity suggest the possibility for a radical reconceptualization of both. Because they provide for a critique of the existing modernist paradigm of education while at the same time holding out the possibility of a more inclusive and egalitarian conception of schooling, they have the potential to make the ambiguous space that teachers occupy between the curriculum and the classroom a more productive ambiguity. And in their understanding of identity formation as a process inseparable from the social, cultural, and political traditions and contexts in which it takes place, postmodernism and hermeneutics open the door to a more authentic and organic understanding of national identity.

Part III: The Power of the Past

Implicit in the narrative of national identity that forms the main portion of this book was an investigation of the evolution of the concept over time. If, as I argue, national identity as it is described in the curriculum is increasingly irrelevant to both teachers and students, the history of its growing irrelevance begs examination. Surprisingly, this examination reveals a history of ambiguous and halting portrayals of Canadian identity, suggesting that from its inception the mythic structure of the nation was fatally flawed by a dependent colonial mentality. The examination further reveals that schools played an active role in passing on and perpetuating a series of frozen tropes of national identity that celebrated a progressively diminishing and irrelevant imperial connection while ignoring the profound social and demographic changes taking place within Canada.

This disjunction between the modernist attempt to manufacture a viable national identity and the nostalgic and ultimately paralyzing longing for the reflected glories of empire has already been noted (Lower 1958). An examination of curriculum documents in Alberta certainly reveals concrete evidence of this split. For example, as late as 1970, students in grade eleven were still busily engaged in examining the intricacies of nineteenth-century British trade policy under the odd and self-serving title "The Modern Background of Canadian Civilization" (Government of Alberta 1965). And while the patent irrelevancy of an analysis of the effect of the Corn Laws on Britain's balance-of-trade situation to the development of Canadian "civilization" is manifest, the psychological impact of the curriculum discourse deserves comment.

Postmodernism suggests that relations of power are built into language and that it is only through careful analysis of linguistic structures that such relations are revealed (Foucault 1972). In terms of the curriculum, both postmodern analysts and reconceptualists alike reject the notion of the neutrality of the curriculum and speak instead of either the "null" curriculum (Eisner 1994) or the "hidden curriculum" (Giroux and Purpel

1983) aimed at the reproduction (and legitimation) of the existing social, political and economic milieu (Bowles and Gintis 1976).

However, beyond simple reproduction is the more critical question of identification. In this sense it is possible to view the Alberta curriculum (at least until 1971) as establishing a symbolic network in which the British tie assumes the status (in Lacanian terms) of the Big Other that simultaneously establishes the discourse around which national identity must be constructed while it delegitimates other possible national identity discourses (Lacan 1977). In this relation, the curriculum frames the fantasy structure of national identity that, in Renata Salecl's (1994) description, constructs "a symbolic space, a point of view, from which we could appear likeable to ourselves" (1994, 33). In many ways, this space is analogous to Homi Bhabha's (1990a) depiction of the nation as a mythic entity that only reaches its horizons "in the mind's eye" (306).

But the critical point, I would argue, is that the fantasy structure of nation as depicted in the Alberta curricula has failed to construct Salecl's welcoming "symbolic space." Corse has noted the possibilities for the construction of a hybrid national identity that takes advantage of

> this long history of tension between an American identity and a British identity, of both reaction against and acceptance of the United States.... Canada was both Old and New World, and its identity lay in both the rejection and the incorporation of some aspects of each. (1997, 57)

However, rather than forming the basis of a truly synthetic and eclectic national identity, the attempt to incorporate what were essentially mutually antagonistic identities into a single Canadian identity resulted in a failure to establish either an enduring mythic structure of national identity or a symbolic space of identification. For these reasons, the modernist attempt to create some kind of "common imagining" of nation through the curriculum failed. As Allen Smith notes in a fitting, if brutally frank, epitaph to the effort to manufacture a viable national identity in Canada:

> To register...the absence of a nationalizing idea in Canada at the exact same moment as we remark the presence of one in the United States is...to look for conditions that might explain this difference. And to do that is to see in an instant that while Americans, historically speaking, possess the principal materials—a common language, shared values, etc. necessary to the building of such an idea—Canadians patently do not. (1994, 10)

But, ironically, this failure presents an opportunity to open another kind of "symbolic space" based on approaching national identity through the lenses of ambiguity and difference.   From this perspective, the emergence of Canada as a pluralistic society has created the chance to move beyond the conflicted view of national identity as finely balanced on the turning point between Britain and the United States.   This opportunity was given formal sanction by the Canadian government's 1971 declaration that Canada was officially multicultural as well as bilingual. More critically, however, pluralism represents a dynamic that continually defines and redefines itself and the nation. It is much less amenable to attempts to render it static and timeless in the same way that the British connection came to be portrayed in the curriculum.

And as far as its presentation in the social studies curriculum from 1971 to the present, it is obvious that pluralism, as a critical aspect of national identity, has assumed an increasingly prominent role.   First described in terms that emphasized its subordinate status to the two founding nations and discussed the "assimilation of *other* [my italics] minorities in either the English or French linguistic groups..." (Government of Alberta 1971, 36), by 1990, multiculturalism was accorded equal status with bilingualism as one of the "fundamental" characteristics of Canadian identity, and pluralism was described as a "value" that all Canadians subscribe to (Government of Alberta 1990, 14). However, the 1990 *Program of Studies* still presented pluralism in unproblematic, contributory, and essentially modernist terms.   These conceptions of multiculturalism were challenged by the discussions that developed in the course of the action research component of this research.

Part IV: Giving Shape to Ambiguity

As I have noted, the action research project that formed the core of this book was a kind of ambiguous and collaborative narrative of national identity.   Homi Bhabha, whose depiction of the hybrid third space of national identity formation, provided us with the location to reimagine national identity, emphasizes this narrative quality as a characteristic of all nations. He notes that "nations, like narratives, lose their origins in the myths of time" and later observes that "to encounter the nation as it is written displays a temporality of culture and social consciousness more in tune with the partial, overdetermined process by which textual meaning is produced" (1990a, 306–7).

In discussing the nation in terms of what is essentially a hermeneutic act of interpretation, Bhabha opens up the possibility of multiple narratives of national identity. Certainly, within our action research group, our own "narrations of the nation" were very divergent. But this wide divergence was expressive of more than differing intellectual formulations of national identity. It was representative of the process of hermeneutically inspired action research that encouraged each of us to reflect on and to share our own sense of identity while discussing the wider issue of the role of education in national identity formation.

From this shared reflection, a sense of collaboration emerged that was founded on what Paul Ricoeur (1981) calls a "hermeneutics of trust" and that Gadamer (1975) describes as "the good will to try to understand one another." The "trust" and "good will" implicit in moderate hermeneutics find their parallel in action research. Carson refers to poststructural action research as a "hermeneutics of practice" that attempts "to attend most carefully to interpreting the way we are with our colleagues and students in schools" (1992, 114).

As an approach to the reimagination of a curriculum of national identity, action research informed by hermeneutics established the conditions that made possible the frank, open, and difficult conversations we engaged in. This openness allowed us to approach the question of how to reformulate a more relevant curriculum of national identity in ways that made us more aware of our own subject positions on the issue and more appreciative of the other subject positions that emerged.

This appreciation was critical, because both the location we spoke from as teachers reflecting on changing the curriculum and the idea of national identity itself were ambiguous. There were few fixed referents as we attempted to formulate a theory of difference that suggested the teaching of radically altered approaches to pluralism and national identity based on postmodern methodologies. I have already noted John's sense of unease at this tenuous position in the introduction to Chapter 2, but he was not alone in his disquiet. As we neared the completion of our examination of Slattery's text, Sunita expressed the concern that "I feel like we're juggling too many balls. We have to fit Taylor's ideas into Slattery's format and then slide the whole thing into the national identity section [of the curriculum]. I hope we can pull this off."

But despite these concerns, we persisted in our efforts. In retrospect, I think the commitment to continue in the face of a very complex task was partially grounded in a postmodern sensibility that "humanity can and must go beyond the modern" (Griffen 1993, vii–viii) and that what we were doing was a legitimate and valuable exercise in the service of that ideal. More than that, however, I think it was grounded in the sense of obligation we had developed toward one another. This sense of obligation certainly reflected our appreciation for the differing subject positions on national identity noted above, but in some ways it also reflected the emergence of a community structured around acceptance of Taylor's notion of deep diversity.

Moving from the sense of community that had emerged within the group to the formulation of a theory of difference that refused to present pluralism in unproblematized terms was, in a sense, a natural process. We had accepted that each of us had a different narrative of national identity, and that it was possible for us to hold differing views on national identity without unduly fragmenting the group. In a sense, Jim's departure was a test of the strength of the "fragile bonds" Caputo (1993) notes. Although we were sometimes at odds, we remained committed to reconceptualizing national identity based on our understanding of Taylor's ambiguous concept of deep diversity and Slattery's postmodern methodology.

Underlying the whole project was our firm belief that national identity formation was an ambiguous and problematic process and that implicit in this process was the critical notion of difference. Any attempt to formulate a curriculum of national identity in plural cultures that ignored this notion risked situating national identity in a modernist paradigm that would tend to portray minority cultures in terms of their contribution to the health and development of the dominant culture (McCarthy 1998).

This emergent conception of the nation as constructed across a "bar of difference" (Bhabha 1990b, 210) has not yet achieved wide acceptance. As Roger Collins notes: "That both cultural differences and social conflict are inherent features of any pluralistic society is a perspective that remains at odds with the mainstream perspective that treats social conflict as social disease" (1993, 202). This equation is founded on the modernist idea that social harmony is the ideal in pluralistic states, but as Chantal Mouffe reminds us, harmony can easily be a mask for assimilation and repression:

Instead of trying to reduce the existing plurality through devices like the veil of ignorance...we need to develop a positive attitude toward differences, even if they lead to conflict and impede the realization of harmony. Any understanding of pluralism whose objective is to reach harmony is ultimately a negation of the positive value of diversity and difference. (1995, 44)

The assignments we designed represented our attempt to leave open and unanswered the question of whether diversity was a positive or negative aspect of national identity. Instead, they pointed to the ambiguous possibilities of pluralism. In grounding students' investigations of identity in individual experience, they reflected a postmodern and hermeneutic sensibility of the legitimacy of autobiography in the identity forming process. Finally, in holding out the possibility of attachments that were wider than the immediate and the personal, they opened a conduit through which students might see themselves and their own narratives situated in the broader narrative of the nation. All of these aspects of a postmodern and hermeneutically inspired curriculum suggest that teachers need to adopt the roles of guide, companion, and mentor as students explore the ambiguous ground of identity formation.

If this book began with absurdity, it ends, appropriately, in ambiguity. This will remain the location that teachers speak from, the terrain that action research occupies, and the site of the enunciation of national identity. It is redolent of the postmodern condition, but it is not the terrain of nihilism, alienation, and despair. With ambiguity, the question of how teachers should approach national identity is not answered with the modernist "final word" that David Jardine warns leads only to silence and alienation (Jardine 1992). Instead, ambiguous conceptions of difference and national identity remain living conceptions able to accommodate the conflict and negotiation typical of plural societies, and, most critically, able to seize the imagination and passion of our students.

NOTES

Chapter 1

1. The phrase is perhaps best translated as "the strand of an identity."

2. See, for example, Francis Fukuyama, *The End of History and the Last Man* (London: Hamish Hamilton, 1992); and Michael Ignatieff, *Blood and Belonging: Journeys into the New Nationalism* (Toronto: Viking Press, 1993).

Chapter 2

1. A number of recent works have ironically speculated on the absence of national identity as a characteristic of Canadian identity. See, for example, Frank Davey, *Post-National Arguments* (Toronto: McClelland and Stewart, 1993); Richard Gwynn, *Nationalism without Walls: The Unbearable Lightness of Being Canadian* (Toronto: McClelland and Stewart, 1995); and Linda Hutcheon, *The Canadian Postmodern: A Study of Contemporary English Canadian Fiction* (London: Oxford University Press, 1988).

Chapter 3

1. There are strong parallels between Pirandello's independent and uncooperative actors and the participants in action research. Both refuse to be bound by the text and both play out their roles in an absurdist "play within a play." See Luigi Pirandello, *Six Characters in Search of an Author* (London: Eyre Methuen, 1979).

2. Martin Esslin defines absurdism as a "sense of the senselessness of the human condition and the inadequacy of the rational approach [characterized] by the open abandonment of rational devices and discursive thought." *The Theatre of the Absurd* (London: Peregrine Books, 1987), 24.

Chapter 4

1. Carl Berger documents the Canada First movement well in *The Sense of Power: Studies in the Ideas of Canadian Imperialism, 1870–1914* (Toronto: University of Toronto Press, 1970).

2. Poststructuralism's problematization of the arbitrary relationship between the signifier (a word or a phrase) and the signified (the concept to which the word refers) suggests that in the symbolic network that links signifier to signified, meaning is determined by use rather than by a fixed set of relationships. See, for example, Dominic Strinati, *An Introduction to Theories of Popular Culture* (London and New York: Routledge, 1995).

3. See, for example, Pierre Berton, *Vimy* (Toronto: McClelland and Stewart, 1986); and Donald Creighton, *Canada's First Century* (Toronto: MacMillan of Canada, 1970).

Chapter 5

1. French linguist Oswald Ducrot discusses the idea that the fantasy of nation must both call out to the people and be recognized by them. For Ducrot, discourse can be meaningful only if the addressee recognizes herself or himself in that discourse. *Le Dire et le Dit* (Paris: Minuit, 1984).

2. In *The Malaise of Modernity,* for example, Taylor warns of the extreme and destructive individualism at the heart of Derrida's "radical, untrammeled sense of freedom." (Concord: House of Anansi Press, 1991), p. 130.

Chapter 6

1. David Levin has written a brilliant description of this appreciation: "Like other moderns, I shall face the future, gazing directly into it. But unlike earlier moderns, I face this future with more confusion, more uncertainty, more self-doubt and more awareness of ambiguities and complexities." "Existentialism at the End of Modernity: Questioning the I's Eyes," *Philosophy Today* (Spring 1990): 83.

REFERENCES

Alejandro, Roberto. 1993. *Hermeneutics, Citizenship and the Public Sphere*. Albany: State University of New York Press.

Altrichter, Herbert, Peter Posch, and Bridgett Somekh. 1993. *Teachers Investigate Their Work: An Introduction to the Methods of Action Research*. New York: Routledge.

Anderson, Benedict. 1995. *Imagined Communities: Reflections on the Origin and Spread of Nationalism*. London: Verso.

Angus, Howard F. 1938. *Canada and Her Great Neighbour*. Toronto, Ontario: Ryerson Press.

Aoki, Douglas. 1996. "The Thing of Culture." *University of Toronto Quarterly* 65, no. 4: 404–18.

Aoki, Ted T. 1988. "Towards a Dialectic between the Conceptual World and the Lived World: Transcending Instrumentalism in Curriculum Orientation." In *Contemporary Curriculum Discourses,* ed. William F. Pinar, 402–6. Scottsdale: Gorsuch Scarisbrick Pub.

———. 1989. "Layered Understandings of Curriculum and Pedagogy: Challenges to Curriculum Developers." Paper presented to the Alberta Teachers Association, Edmonton, Alberta, Canada, March.

———. 1992. "Layered Voices of Teaching: The Uncannily Correct and the Elusively True." In *Understanding Curriculum as Phenomenological and Deconstructed Text,* ed. William F. Pinar and William Reynolds, 17–27. New York: Teachers College

Aoki, Ted T., Walter Werner, Bob Connors, and John Dahlie. 1977. *Whose Culture? Whose Heritage? Ethnicity within Canadian Social Studies Curricula*. Vancouver: Centre for the Study of Curriculum and Instruction.

Apple, Michael W. 1978. "The New Sociology of Education: Analyzing Cultural and Economic Reproduction." *Harvard Educational Review* 48, no. 4: 495–503.

———. 1993. *Official Knowledge: Democratic Education in a Conservative Age*. New York: Routledge.

———. 1998. *The Curriculum: Problems, Politics, and Possibilities*. Albany: State University of New York Press.

Aronowitz, Stanley, and Henry Giroux. 1991. *Postmodern Education: Politics, Culture and Social Criticism*. Minneapolis: University of Minneapolis Press.

Balibar, Etienne. 1995. "Culture and Identity (Working Notes)." In *The Identity in Question,* ed. John Rajchman, 173–198. New York: Routledge.

Barber, Benjamin. 1984. *Strong Democracy: Participatory Politics for a New Age*. Berkeley: University of California Press.

———. 1995. *Jihad vs. McWorld*. New York: Random House.

Barthes, Roland. 1988. *The Semiotic Challenge*. Oxford: Blackwell.

Beck, Clive. 1997. *Postmodernism, Pedagogy, and Philosophy of Education* (p. 112) http://www.ed.uiuc.edu/COE/EPS/PES-yearbook/93_docs/BECK.HTM.

Beckett, Samuel. 1958. *Endgame*. New York: Grove Press.

———. 1959a. *Waiting for Godot*. London: Faber and Faber.

————. 1959b. *The Unnamable*. London: John Calder.

Bennett, Richard B. 1928. "Debate: Immigration (June 7)." In *House of Commons Debates, 3rd Parliament, 2nd Session–18th Parliament, 2nd Session*. Vol. 1: 1875–1937, 3925–27.

Berger, Carl. 1970. *The Sense of Power: Studies in the Ideas of Canadian Imperialism, 1867–1914*. Toronto: University of Toronto Press.

Bercovitch, Sacvan. 1993. *The Rights of Assent: Transformations in the Symbolic Construction of America*. New York: Routledge.

Bernard, Hilly. 1994. *Hermeneutics and Education: Discourse/Practice*. Unpublished Book Prospectus. New Orleans: University of New Orleans.

Berton, Pierre. 1986. *Vimy*. Toronto: McClelland and Stewart.

Beyer, Landon F., and Daniel P. Liston. 1996. *Curriculum in Conflict: Social Visions, Educational Agendas, and Progressive School Reform*. New York: Teachers College Press.

Bhabha, Homi K. 1990a. "The Third Space: An Interview with Homi Bhabha." In *Identity, Community, Culture, Difference*, ed. John Rutherford, 201–13. London: Lawrence and Wishert.

————. 1990b. "Narrating the Nation." In *The Nation and Narration*, ed. Homi K. Bhabha, 306–12. London: Routledge.

————. 1995. "Freedom's Basis in the Indeterminate." In *The Identity in Question*, ed. John Rajchman, 47–62. New York: Routledge.

Blacker, David. 1993. "Education as the Normative Dimension of Philosophical Hermeneutics." Paper presented at the annual meeting of the Philosophy of Education Society, New Orleans, Louisiana, April.

Bleicher, John. 1980. *Contemporary Hermeneutics: Hermeneutics as Method, Philosophy, and Critique*. London: Routledge and Kegan Paul.

Boii, Larry. 1993. *Trying to Teach: Interim Report of the Committee on Public Education*. Edmonton, Alberta: The Alberta Teachers Association.

Borgmann, Albert. 1992. *Crossing the Postmodern Divide*. Chicago: University of Chicago Press.

Bourdieu, Pierre, and Jean C. Passeron. 1977. *Reproduction in Education, Society and Culture*. Trans. Robert Nice. London: Sage Publications.

Bowles, Samuel, and Herbert Gintis. 1976. *Schooling in Capitalist America*. New York: Basic Books.

Braudel, Fernand. 1988. *L'identité de la France: Espace et Histoire*. Paris: Arthaud Flammarion.

Britzman, Deborah P. 1991. *Practice Makes Practice: A Critical Study of Learning to Teach*. Albany: State University of New York Press.

Brock, Colin, and Witold Tulasiewicz. 1985. *Cultural Identity and Educational Policy*. London: Croom Helm.

Brock-Utne, Birgit. 1988. "What Is Educational Action Research?" In *The Action Research Reader*, ed. Stephen Kemmis and Robin McTaggart, 253–58. 3rd ed. Victoria, British Columbia: Deakin University.

Burke, James. 1941. "An Analysis of the Social Studies 3 Examination Paper of June, 1940." M.A. thesis, University of Alberta.

Bussard, Leonard H. 1944. "A Comparative Study of Social Studies Achievement of Canadian Grade XI Students." M.Ed. thesis, University of Alberta.

Cairns, Alan. 1993. "The Fragmentation of Canadian Citizenship." In *Belonging: The Meaning and Future of Canadian Citizenship,* ed. William Kaplan, 68–82. Montreal: McGill-Queens University Press.

Callan, Eamonn. 1994. "Beyond Sentimental Civic Education." *American Journal of Education* 102 (February): 190–221.

Camus, Albert. 1975. *The Myth of Sysyphus.* London: Penguin.

Canetti, Elias. 1973. *Crowds and Power.* London: Penguin.

Caputo, John D. 1987. *Radical Hermeneutics: Repetition, Deconstruction, and the Hermeneutic Project.* Bloomington: Indiana University Press.

———. 1993. *Against Ethics: Contributions to a Poetics of Obligation with Constant Reference to Deconstruction.* Bloomington: Indiana University Press.

Carr, William, and Stephen Kemmis. 1983. *Becoming Critical: Knowing through Action Research.* Victoria: Deakin University Press.

Carson, Terrance R. 1989. "Collaboratively Inquiring into Action Research." In *Exploring Collaborative Action Research,* ed. Terrance R. Carson and Dennis Sumara, i–ix. Proceedings of the Ninth Invitational Conference of the Canadian Association for Curriculum Studies. Jasper, Alberta: Canadian Association for Curriculum Studies.

Carson, Terrance R. 1992. "Remembering Forward: Reflections on Education for Peace." In *Understanding Curriculum as Phenomenological and Deconstructed Text,* ed. William. F. Pinar and William M. Reynolds, 102–15. New York: Teachers College Press.

———. 1994. "Not Ethics but Obligation: Reflections on Collaborative Teaching and Research." Paper presented to the Eighth International Conference on Korean Studies, Seoul, Korea, April.

Carson, Terrance R., and Dennis Sumara. 1997. "Editors' Introduction: Reconceptualizing Action Research as a Living Practice." In *Action Research as a Living Practice,* ed. Terrance R. Carson and Dennis Sumara, xiii–xxxv. New York: Peter Lang Publishing.

Castenell, Louis, and William F. Pinar, ed. 1993. *Understanding Curriculum as Racial Text: Representations of Identity and Difference in Education.* Albany: State University of New York Press.

Chaiton, Alph, and Neil McDonald. 1977. *Canadian Schools and Canadian Identity.* Toronto: Gage.

Cobban, Andrew. 1964. *Rousseau and the Modern State.* London: George Allen and Unwin.

Cochrane, Charles N., and William S. Wallace. 1926. *This Canada of Ours.* Toronto: National Council on Education.

Collins, Roger. 1993. "Responding to Cultural Diversity in Our Schools." In *Understanding Curriculum as Racial Text: Representations of Identity and Difference in Education,* ed. Louis Castenell and William. F. Pinar, 195–208. Albany: State University of New York Press.

Committee for the Study of Canadian History Textbooks. 1945. *Canadian Education: Report of the Committee for the Study of Canadian History Textbooks.* Toronto: Canadian Education Association.

Connelly, F. Michael, and D. Jean Clandinin. 1999. *Shaping a Professional Identity: Stories of Educational Practice.* New York: Teachers College Press.

Cook, Ramsay, John T. Ricker and John Saywell. 1964. *Canada: A Modern Nation.* Toronto: Clarke Irwin.

Corse, Sarah M. 1997. *Nationalism and Literature: The Politics of Culture in Canada and the United States.* Cambridge: University of Cambridge Press.

Couture, Jean-Claude. 1997. "Impaired Driving." In *Action Research as a Living Practice,* ed. Terrance R. Carson and Dennis Sumara, 109–20. New York: Peter Lang Publishing.

———. 1999. "The Gift of Failure: Teacher Commitment in the Postmodern Classroom." Ph.D. diss., University of Alberta.

Creighton, Donald G. 1970. *Canada's First Century.* Toronto: Macmillan of Canada.

Cubberly, Ellwood. 1929. *Public Schools Administration.* Boston: Houghton Mifflin.

Davey, Frank. 1993. *Post-National Arguments.* Toronto: McClelland and Stewart.

Deleuze, Gilles, and Clare Parnet. 1977. *Dialogues.* Paris: Flammarion.

Derrida, Jacques. 1993. "Discussion: Structure, Sign and Play in the Discourse of the Human Sciences." In *A Postmodern Reader,* ed. Joseph Natoli and Linda Hutcheon, 223–42. Albany: State University of New York Press. Baltimore: Johns Hopkins University Press.

Doll, William E. 1993. *A Post-modern Perspective on Curriculum.* New York: Teachers College Press.

Donald, James, and Ali Rattansi, ed. 1992. *"Race," Culture, and Difference.* London: Sage Publications.

"Dominion Institute Releases History Poll Results," *Edmonton Journal,* June 20, 2000, p. A-14.

Ducrot, Oswald. 1984. *Le Dire et le Dit.* Paris: Minuit.

Eagleton, Terry. 1996. *The Illusions of Postmodernism.* London: Blackwell.

Eco, Umberto. 1983. *The Name of the Rose.* New York: Harcourt, Brace, Jovanovich.

———. 1994. *Six Walks in the Fictional Woods.* Cambridge: Harvard University Press.

"Editorial." *Edmonton Bulletin.* August 15, 1892, p. 3.

Edgerton, Susan H. 1991. "Particularities of 'Otherness': Autobiography, Maya Angelou, and Me." In *Curriculum as Social Psychoanalysis: The Significance of Place,* ed. Joe Kinchloe and William F. Pinar, 77–98. Albany: State University of New York Press.

Eisner, Elliott. 1994. *The Educational Imagination.* 3rd ed. New York: Macmillan.

Elliott, John. 1991. *Action Research for Educational Change.* Milton Keynes: Open University Press.

Esslin, Martin. 1987. *The Theatre of the Absurd.* 3rd ed. London: Peregrine.

Fitzgerald, Thomas K. 1993. *Metaphors of Identity: A Culture-Communication Dialogue.* Albany: State University of New York Press.

Flax, Jane. 1990. *Thinking Fragments. Psychoanalysis, Feminism, and Postmodernism in the Contemporary West.* Berkeley: University of California Press.

Foucault, Michel. 1972. *The Archaeology of Knowledge and the Discourse on Language.* Trans. Alan M. Sheridan. New York: Pantheon.

———. 1980. *Power/Knowledge: Selected Interviews and Other Writings 1972–77,*ed. Colin Gordon. New York: Pantheon.

Fukuyama, Francis. 1992. *The End of History and the Last Man.* London: Hamish Hamilton.

Fullan, Michael. 1991. *The Meaning of Educational Change.* Toronto: OISE Press.

Gadamer, Hans-Georg. 1975. *Truth and Method.* New York: Crossroad.

———. 1976. *Philosophical Hermeneutics.* Trans. and ed. D. Linge. Berkeley: University of California Press.

———. 1979. Practical Philosophy as a Model of the Human Sciences. *Research in Phenomenology* IX: 74–85

Gallagher, Shaun. 1992. *Hermeneutics and Education.* Albany: State University of New York Press.

Gauthier, Clement. 1992. "Between Crystal and Smoke or, How to Miss the Point in the Debate about Action Research." In *Understanding Curriculum as Phenomenological and Deconstructed Text,* ed. William. F. Pinar and William Reynolds. New York: Teachers College Press. 184–94.

Gellner, Ernest. 1983. *Nations and Nationalism.* Oxford: Blackwell. 1983.

———. 1994. *Encounters with Nationalism.* Oxford: Blackwell.

Ghosh, Ratna. 1996. *Redefining Multicultural Education.* Toronto: Harcourt Brace.

Ghosh, Ratna, and Douglas Ray, ed. 1987. *Social Change and Education in Canada.* Toronto: Harcourt, Brace Jovanovich.

Giddens, Anthony. 1990. *The Consequences of Modernity.* Stanford: Stanford University Press.

Giroux, Henry. 1983. *Theory and Resistance in Education: A Pedagogy for the Opposition.* South Hadley: Bergin and Garvey.

———. 1988. *Schooling and the Struggle for Public Life: Critical Pedagogy in the Modern Age.* Minneapolis: University of Minnesota Press.

———. 1993a. *Living Dangerously: Multiculturalism and the Politics of Difference.* New York: Peter Lang.

———. 1993b. "Postmodernism as Border Pedagogy: Redefining theBoundaries of Race and Ethnicity." In *A Postmodern Reader,* ed. J. Napoli and Linda Hutcheon, 452–96. Albany: State University of New York Press.

———. 1996. *Counternarratives: Cultural Studies and Critical Pedagogies in Postmodern Spaces.* New York, Routledge.

Giroux, Henry, ed. 1991. *Postmodernism, Feminism and Cultural Politics: Redrawing Educational Boundaries.* Albany: State University of New York Press.

Giroux, Henry, and David Purpel, ed. 1983. *The Hidden Curriculum and Moral Education.* Berkeley, California: McCutchan.

Goggin, Donald J. 1906. "Northwest Autonomy." In *Empire Club Speeches.* 212–13. Toronto: Queen's Printers.

Government of Alberta. 1939. *Program of Studies for the High School.* Edmonton: King's Printers.

———. 1955. *Senior High School Curriculum Guide.* Edmonton: Department of Education.

————. 1965. *Senior High School Curriculum Guide.* Edmonton: Department of Education.

————. 1971. *Social Studies Program.* Edmonton: Department of Education.

————. 1981. *Alberta Social Studies Curriculum.* Edmonton: Alberta Education.

————. 1985. *Canadian Awareness Project Report.* Edmonton: Alberta Education.

————. 1990. *Alberta Social Studies Curriculum.* Edmonton: Alberta Education.

Government of Canada. 1962. *Canada: Census 1961.* Ottawa: Dominion Bureau of Statistics.

————. 1972. *Canada: Census 1971.* Ottawa: Statistics Canada.

————. 1982. *Canada: Census 1981.* Ottawa: Statistics Canada.

————. 1992. *Canada: Census 1991.* Ottawa: Statistics Canada.

————. 2000. *What Is Multiculturalism? National Conference on Immigration.* Ottawa: Canadian Heritage. (pp.1–7) http://www.pch.gc.ca/multi/what-multi_e.shtml.

Granatstein, Jack. A. 1998. *Who Killed Canadian History.* Toronto: HarperCollins.

Grant, Carl A., and Judyth. M. Sachs. 1995. "Multicultural Education and Postmodernism: Movement toward a Dialogue." In *Critical Multiculturalism: Uncommon Voices in a Common Struggle,* ed. Barry Kanpol and Peter McLaren, 89–106. Westport: Bergin and Garvey.

Grant, George M. 1965. *Lament for a Nation: The Defeat of Canadian Nationalism.* Toronto: McClelland and Stewart.

Greene, Maxine. 1997. *The Plays and Ploys of Postmodernism.* (pp. 1–6) http://www.ed.uiuc.edu/COE/EPS/PES-yearbook/93_docs/GREENE.HTM.

Griffen, David R. 1993. *Founders of Constructive Postmodern Philosophy: Pierce, James, Bergson, Whitehead, and Hartshorne.* Albany: State University of New York Press.

Grumet, Madeleine R. 1988. *Bitter Milk: Women and Teaching:* Amherst: University of Massachusetts Press.

Grundy, Shirley, and Stephen Kemmis. 1988. "Educational Action Research in Australia: The State of the Art." In *The Action Research Reader,* ed. Stephen Kemmis and Robin McTaggart, 321–26. 3rd ed. Victoria: Deakin University Press.

Guttieriez, Kris, and Peter McLaren. 1995. "Pedagogies of Dissent and Transformation: A Dialogue about Postmodernism, Social Context and the Politics of Literacy." In *Critical Multiculturalism: Uncommon Voices in a Common Struggle,* ed. B. Kanpol and P. McLaren, 125–48. Westport: Bergin and Garvey.

Gwynn, Richard. 1995. *Nationalism without Walls: The Unbearable Lightness of Being Canadian.* Toronto: McClelland and Stewart.

Habermas, Jürgen. 1970. *Knowledge and Human Interests.* Boston: Beacon Press.

————. 1984. *The Theory of Communicative Interest: Reason and the Rationalization of Society.* Boston: Beacon Press.

Hall, Stuart. 1981. "Cultural Studies: Two Paradigms." In *Culture, Ideology and Social Process,* ed. T. Bennett, et al. Milton Keynes: Open University Press.

————. 1991. "The Local and the Global." In *Culture, Globalisation, and the World System: Contemporary Conditions for Representations of Identity,* ed. A. King, 19–40. Albany: State University of New York Press.

Harvey, David. 1989. *The Condition of Postmodernity.* Oxford: Basil Blackwell.

Hegel, Georg W. F. 1975. *Lectures on the Philosophy of World History.* Cambridge: Cambridge University Press.

Heller, Agnes. 1993. "Existentialism, Alienation, Postmodernism: Cultural Movements as Vehicles of Change in the Patterns of Everyday Life." In *A Postmodern Reader,* ed. Joseph Natoli and Linda Hutcheon, 497–509. Albany: State University of New York Press.

Hobsbawm, Eric. 1992. *Nations and Nationalism Since 1870: Programme, Myth, Reality,* Cambridge: Cambridge University Press.

Hobsbawm, Eric, and Terence Ranger. 1983. *The Invention of Tradition.* Cambridge: Cambridge University Press.

Hodgetts, A. B. 1968. *What Culture? What Heritage?* Toronto: OISE Press.

Hodgetts, A. B., and Paul Gallagher. 1978. *Teaching Canada for the 1980's.* Toronto: OISE Press.

Hoffman, Diane. 1996. "Culture and Self in Multicultural Education: Reflections on Discourse, Text and Practice." *American Educational Research Journal.* 33, no. 3: 545–69.

Hollins, Etta R., ed. 1996. *Transforming Curriculum for a Culturally Diverse Society.* Mahwah, New Jersey: Lawrence Erlbaum Associates.

Houtekamer, Tweela, Cynthia Chambers, Rochelle Yamagishi, and Evelyn Good Striker. 1997. "Exploring Sacred Relations: Collaborative Action Research." In *Action Research as a Living Practice,* ed. Terrance. R. Carson and Dennis Sumara, 137–60. New York: Peter Lang Publishing.

Howard, R. J. 1982. *Three Faces of Hermeneutics.* Berkeley: University of California Press.

Hubbell, Jay B. 1972. *Who Are the Major American Writers? A Study of the Changing Literary Canon.* Durham, North Carolina: Duke University Press.

Hutcheon, Linda. 1988. *The Canadian Postmodern: A Study of Contemporary English-Canadian Fiction.* Oxford: Oxford University Press.

Huyssen, Andreas. 1995. "The Inevitability of Nation: German after Unification." In *The Identity in Question,* ed. John. Rajchman, 73–92. London: Routledge.

Ignatieff, Michael. 1993. *Blood and Belonging: Journeys into the New Nationalism.* Toronto: Viking Press.

———. 2000. *The Rights Revolution.* Toronto: House of Anansi Press.

Jameson, Anna B. 1972. *Winter Studies and Summer Rambles in Canada.* Toronto: Coles Publishing Company.

Jameson, Frederic. 1991. *Postmodernism and the Cultural Logic of Late Capitalism.* Durham, North Carolina: Duke University Press.

Jardine, David W. 1992. "Reflections on Education, Hermeneutics, and Ambiguity: Hermeneutics as a Restoring of Life to Its Original Difficulty." In *Understanding Curriculum as Phenomenological and Deconstructed Text,* ed. William. F. Pinar and William Reynolds, 116–30. New York: Teachers College Press.

Kanpol, Barry, and Peter McLaren. 1995. "Introduction: Resistance, Multiculturalism, and the Politics of Difference." In *Critical Multiculturalism: Uncommon Voices in a Common Struggle,* ed. Barry. Kanpol and Peter McLaren, 1–18. Westport: Bergin and Garvey.

Kemmis, Stephen. 1988. "Action Research in Retrospect and Prospect." In *The Action Research Reader*, ed. Stephen Kemmis and Robin McTaggert, 27–40. 3rd ed. Victoria: Deakin University Press.

Kemmis, Stephen, and Robin McTaggert,eds. 1988. *The Action Research Reader*. 3rd ed. Victoria: Deakin University Press.

Kerby, Anthony. 1991. *Narrative and Self.* Bloomington: Indiana University Press.

Kinchloe, Joe, and William. F. Pinar, eds., 1991. *Curriculum as Social Psychological Analysis: The Significance of Place.* Albany: State University of New York Press.

Klafki, Wolfgang. 1988. "Decentralized Curriculum Development in the Form of Action Research." In *The Action Research Reader*, ed. Stephen Kemmis and Robin McTaggert, 235–244. 3rd ed. Victoria: Deakin University Press.

Kristeva, Julia. 1991. *Strangers to Ourselves.* Trans. Leon S. Roudiez. New York: Columbia University Press.

———. 1993. *Nations without Nationalism.* Trans. Leon S. Roudiez. New York: Columbia University Press.

Kymlicka, Will. 1989. *Liberalism, Community, and Culture.* Oxford: Oxford University Press.

———. 1992. *Recent Work in Citizenship Theory.* Ottawa: Multiculturalism and Citizenship Canada.

———. 1995. *Multicultural Citizenship.* Oxford: Oxford University Press.

Lacan, Jacques. 1972. *Écrits: A Selection.* Trans. Alan Sheridan. London: Tavistock Press.

Laclau, Ernesto. 1977. *Politics and Ideology in Marxist Theory: Capitalism, Fascism, Populism.*London: New Left Books.

———. 1988. "Politics and the Limits of Modernity." In *Universal Abandon: The Politics of Postmodernism*, ed. A. Ross. Minneapolis: University of Minnesota Press.

Lasch, Christopher. 1984. *The Minimal Self: Psychic Survival in Troubled Times.*New York: Norton.

Lather, Patti. 1991. *Getting Smart: Feminist Research and Pedagogy with/in the Postmodern.* New York: Routledge.

Laxer, Robert M. 1969. "Identity and Canadian Studies." In *The Canadian National Identity,* ed. E. D. Humphrey, 109–21. Toronto: OISE

Levin, David. M. 1990. "Existentialism at the End of Modernity: Questioning the I's Eyes." *Philosophy Today* (Spring): 80–95.

Lewin, Kurt. 1988. "Action Research and Minority Problems." In *The Action Research Reader,* ed. Stephen. Kemmis and Robin McTaggert, 41–46. 3rd ed. Victoria: Deakin University Press.

Lower, Arthur R. 1959. *Canadians in the Making.* Toronto: Longmans.

Lupul, Manoly. 1977. "Multiculturalism and Canadian National Identity: The Alberta Experience." In *Canadian Schools and Canadian Identity* ed. Alph Chaiton and Neil McDonald, 165–75. Toronto: Gage Educational Publishing.

Lyotard, Jean-Francois. 1993. "Excerpts from the Postmodern Condition: A Report on Knowledge." In *A Postmodern Reader,* ed. Joseph Natoli and Linda Hutcheon, 71–90. Minneapolis: University of Minnesota Press.

Madison, Gary B. 1988. *The Hermeneutics of Postmodernity: Figures and Themes.* Bloomington: Indiana University Press.

Mallea, John. R. 1989. *Schooling in a Plural Canada.* Exeter, U.K.: Short Run Press.

Martin, A. K. 1999. "Towards an Epistemology of Professionalism: Perturbations, Metaphors, and Politics." Paper presented at the Annual Meeting of the Canadian Society for Studies in Education, June.

Matore, Georges, and Madeleine Eristov, eds. 1980. *Textes D'étude: XIXe-XXe Siècles.* Paris: Société Saint-Quentinoise d'Imprimerie.

McCarthy, Cameron. 1998. *The Uses of Culture.* New York: Routledge.

McCrone, Donald. 1992. *Understanding Scotland: The Sociology of a Stateless Nation.* London: Routledge.

McInnis, Edgar. 1969. *Canada.* 3rd ed. Toronto: Holt, Rinehart and Winston of Canada.

McLellan, James A. 1878. "President's Address." *Proceedings of the Ontario Teachers' Association.* Toronto: Queen's Printers.

Megill, Alan. 1985. *Prophets of Extremity.* Berkeley: University of California Press.

Michelet, Jules. 1973. *The People.* Trans. John P. McKay. Chicago: University of Illinois Press.

Michelfelder, Diane. 1989. "Derrida and the Ethics of the Ear." In *The Question of the Other: Essays in Contemporary Continental Philosophy,* ed. A. Dallery and C. Scott, 47–54. Albany: State University of New York Press.

Misgeld, Dieter. 1983. "Phenomenology, Social Science and Social Service Professions: The Case for the Integration of Phenomenology, Hermeneutics and Critical Social Theory (A Reply to Luckmann and Giorgi)." *Phenomenology and Pedagogy* 1, no. 2: 195–14.

Misgeld, Dieter, and David Jardine. 1989. "Hermeneutics as the Undisciplined Child: Hermeneutic and Technical Images of Education." In *Entering the Circle: Hermeneutic Inquiry in Psychology,* ed. M. Packer and R. Addison, 218–40. Albany: State University of New York Press.

Mohanty, S. P. 1989. "Us and Them: In the Philosophical Bases of Political Criticism." *Yale Journal of Criticism* 2 (Spring): 7–19.

Mouffe, Chantal. 1995. "Democratic Politics and the Question of Identity." In *The Identity in Question,* ed. John Rajchman, 33–46. London: Routledge.

Mulvey, Laura. 1986. Magnificent Obsession. *Parachute* 42: 7–12.

Murphy, Rex. 1997. "National Identity." (Canadian Broadcasting Corporation Television Series).

[*New Yorker*]. 1975. *The New Yorker Album of Drawings 1925–75.* New York: Viking Press.

Oliver, Donald W., and Kathleen. W. Gershman, eds. 1989. *Education, Modernity, and Fractured Meaning: Toward a Process Theory of Teaching and Learning.* Albany: State University of New York Press.

Palmer, Howard, ed. 1975. *Immigration and the Rise of Multiculturalism.* Toronto: Copp Clark.

Parsons, Jim, Geoff Milburn, and Max van Manen. 1993. *A Canadian Social Studies.* Edmonton, Alberta: Publication Services, University of Alberta.

Peirce, Bonny N. 1995. "Learning the Hard Way: Maria's Story." In *Critical Multiculturalism: Uncommon Voices in a Common Struggle,* ed. Barry Kanpol and Peter McLaren, 165–96. Westport: Bergin and Garvey.

Peller, Gary. 1987. "Reason and the Mob: The Politics of Representation." *Tikkun* 2, no. 3: 22–34.

Pinar, William F., and Madeleine Grumet. 1976. *Toward a Poor Curriculum.* Dubuque: Kendall/Hunt.

Pinar, William F., ed. 1988. *Contemporary Curriculum Discourses.* Scottsdale, Arizona: Gorsuch, Scarisbrick.

Pinar, William F., and William Reynolds, eds. 1992. *Understanding Curriculum as Phenomenological and Deconstructed Text.* London: Teachers College Press.

Pinar, William F., and Louis Castenell, eds. 1993. *Understanding Curriculum as Racial Text: Representation of Identity and Difference in Education.* Albany: State University of New York Press.

Pinter, Harold. 1961. *The Dwarfs.* London: Methuen.

Pirandello, Luigi. 1979. *Six Characters in Search of an Author.* London: Eyre Methuen.

Ricoeur, Paul. 1981. "The Task of Hermeneutics." In *Paul Ricoeur, Hermeneutics and the Human Sciences,* ed. J. Thompson. Cambridge: Cambridge University Press.

Rorty, Richard. 1987. "Science as Solidarity." In *The Rhetoric of the Human Sciences,* ed. John S. Nelson, Allen Megill, and David N. McCloskey, 38–52. Madison: University of Wisconsin Press, 1987.

———. 1989. *Contingency, Irony, Solidarity.* Cambridge: Cambridge University Press.

———. 1992. *The Linguistic Turn: Essays in Philosophical Method.* Chicago: University of Chicago Press.

———. 1997. "Hermenutics and Education." In *Classic and Contemporary Readings in the Philosophy of Education,* ed. Steven M. Cahn, 522–35 New York: McGraw Hill.

Ryerson, Edgerton. 1868. "The True Principles upon Which a Comprehensive System of National Education Should Be Founded." In *Documentary History of Education in Upper Canada,* ed. James G. Hodgins. Vol. XX. Toronto: Queen's Printers.

Said, Edward W. 1994. *Orientalism.* New York: Vintage.

Salecl, Renata. 1994. *The Spoils of Freedom: Psychoanalysis and Feminism after the Fall of Socialism.* London: Routledge.

Sanford, Nevitt. 1988. "Whatever Happened to Action Research?" In *The Action Research Reader,* ed. Stephen. Kemmis and Robin McTaggart, 127–36. 3rd ed. Victoria: Deakin University Press.

Saul, John R. 1993. *Voltaire's Bastards: The Dictatorship of Reason in the West.* Toronto: Penguin.

Schon, Donald. 1991. *The Reflective Turn: Case Studies in and on Educational Practice.* New York: Teachers College Press.

Schubert, William. 1986. *Curriculum: Perspective, Paradigm, and Possibility.* New York: Macmillan Publishing Co.

Schwab, Joseph. 1996. "The Practical 4: Something for Curriculum Professors to Do." In *Transforming Curriculum for a Culturally Diverse Society,* ed. Etta R. Hollins, 89–118. Mahwah, New Jersey: Lawrence Erlbaum Associates.

Scott, Joan. 1995. "Multiculturalism and the Politics of Identity." In *The Identity in Question,* ed.John Rajchman, 3–14. New York: Routledge.

Sears, Alan. 1996–97. "In Canada Even History Divides: Unique Features of Canadian Citizenship." *International Journal of Social Education* 11, no. 2: 53–67.

Shumsky, Abraham. 1988. "Cooperation in Action Research: A Rationale." In *The Action Research Reader,* ed. Stephen Kemmis and Robin McTaggart, 81–84. 3rd ed. Victoria: Deakin University Press.

Simon, Roger I. 1992. *Teaching against the Grain: Texts for a Pedagogy of Possibility.* Toronto: OISE Press.

Skrtic, Thomas. 1995. *Disability and Democracy: Reconstructing (Special) Education for Postmodernity.* New York: Teachers College Press.

Slattery, Patrick. 1995. *Curriculum Development in the Postmodern Era.* New York: Garland Publishing.

Sloterdijk, P. 1987. *Critique of Cynical Reason.* Minneapolis: University of Minnesota Press.

Smith, Alan. 1994. *Canada—An American Nation? Essays on Continentalism, Identity, and the Canadian Frame of Mind.* Montreal: McGill-Queen's University Press.

Smith, David G. 1989. "Modernism, Post-modernism and the Future of Pedagogy." A paper presented under the auspices of the Canadian Studies Program at The Institute of East and West Studies, Yonsei University, Seoul.

———. 1991. "Hermeneutic Inquiry: The Hermeneutic Imagination and the Pedagogical Text." In *Forms of Curriculum Inquiry,* ed. E. Short, 187–209. Albany: State University of New York Press

———. 1995. "Interpreting Educational Reality." In *Hermeneutics in Educational Discourse,* ed. H. Danner. Durban, South Africa: Butterworth Press.

Smolicz, Jerzy. 1996. "Multiculturalism and an Overarching Framework of Values: Some Educational Responses for Ethnically Plural Societies." In *Transforming Curriculum for a Culturally Diverse Society,* ed. Etta R. Hollins, 59–74. Mahwah, New Jersey: Lawrence Erlbaum Associates.

Spivak, Gyatri C. 1985. "The Rani of Sirmur." In *Europe and Its Others: Proceedings of the Essex Conference on the Sociology of Literature, July, 1984,* ed. Fred. Barker. Colchester: University of Essex.

———. 1987. *In Other Worlds: Essays in Cultural Politics.* London: Methuen.

Stamp, Robert. M. 1977. "Canadian Education and the National Identity." In *Canadian Schools and Canadian Identity,* ed. Alf Chaiton and Neil McDonald 29–37. Toronto: Gage Educational Publishing.

Strinati, Dominic. 1996. *An Introduction to the Theories of Popular Culture.* London: Routledge.

Sumara, Dennis J., and Brent Davis. 1997. "Enlarging the Space of the Possible: Complexity, Complicity, and Action Research Practices." In *Action Research as a Living Practice,* ed. Terrance R. Carson and Dennis Sumara, 299–312. New York: Peter Lang Publishers.

Taba, Hilda, and Elizabeth Noel. 1988. "Steps in the Action Research Process." In *The Action Research Reader,* ed. Stephen Kemmis and Robin McTaggart, 67–74. 3rd ed. Victoria: Deakin University Press.

Tarnopolsky, Walter S. 1975. "The New Policy of Multiculturalism for Canada." In *Immigration and the Rise of Multiculturalism,* ed. Howard Palmer, 143–44. Toronto: Copp Clark.

Taubman, Peter. 1992. "Achieving the Right Distance" In *Understanding Curriculum as Phenomenological and Deconstructed Text,* ed. William F. Pinar and William Reynolds, 216–36. New York: Teachers College Press.

Taylor, Charles. 1989. *Sources of Self: The Making of Modern Identity.* Cambridge: Harvard University Press.

———. 1991. *The Malaise of Modernity.* Concord: House of Anansi Press.

———. 1993. *Reconciling the Solitudes: Essays on Canadian Federalism and Nationalism.* Montreal: McGill-Queen's University Press.

Tiffin, Chris, and Alan Lawson, ed. 1994. *De-scribing Empire: Post-colonialism and Textuality.* London: Routledge.

Titley, E. Brian, and Peter J. Miller, eds. 1982. *Education in Canada: An Interpretation.* Calgary, Alberta: Destselig Enterprises.

Tomkins, George. 1977. "Canadian Education and the Development of a National Consciousness: Historical and Contemporary Perspectives." In *Canadian Schools and Canadian Identity,* ed. Alf Chaiton and Neil McDonald, 6–28. Toronto: Gage Educational Publishing.

Walkerdine, Valerie. 1986. "Progressive Pedagogy and Political Struggle." *Screen* 27, no. 5: 54–60.

Webber, Jeremy. 1994. *Reimagining Canada: Language, Culture, Community and the Canadian Constitution.* Montreal: McGill-Queen's University Press.

Weber, Eugen. 1976. *Peasants into Frenchmen: The Modernisation of Rural France, 1870–1914.* Stanford: Stanford University Press.

Williams, Raymond. 1981. *The Sociology of Culture.* New York: Schocken Books.

Woodsworth, J. S. 1972. *Strangers within Our Gates.* Toronto: University of Toronto Press.

Zizek, Slavoj. 1989. *The Sublime Object of Ideology.* London: Verso.

———. 1996. "Fantasy as a Political Category: A Lacanian Approach." *JPCS: Journal for the Psychoanalysis of Popular Culture and Society* 1, no. 2: 77–85.

INDEX

on border pedagogy, 18–19, 105,
124
on cultural assumptions, 5, 50
on emancipatory postmodernism,
17–18, 71
on modernist education, 54
on postmodernist education, 16,
121, 137–38
on sense of ambiguity in teachers,
27, 135
Goggin, Arthur, 60
Good Canadian
attempts to create, 56, 82–84, 102
as defined by Massey, 51–52, 65
reimagining the, 88–89, 102, 124–
29, 130–33
See also entries beginning with
Program; *entries beginning with*
Social Studies; modernism and
national identity; multiculturalism;
national identity
Good Striker, Evelyn, 89
Granatstein, J. M., 82, 101
Grant, Carl A., 73, 103, 115
Grant, George M., 56
Greene, Maxine, 10
Greenfield, Leah, 81
Griffin, David Ray, 11, 142
Grumet, Madeleine R.
on autobiography in curriculum, 30,
119, 121
on *currere* concept, 19, 120
on education as process, 118
on identity formation, 32
on presence of absence, 133
Grundy, Shirley, 33
Gutierrez, Kris, 73
Gwynn, Richard, 69

H
Habermas, Jürgen, 33, 52
Haliburton, R. G., 55
Hall, Stuart, 19, 115
Harvey, David, 10, 15
Hegel, Georg W. F., 53–54
Heller, Agnes, 12

Heritage Days, 103, 105
hermeneutic circle
author's role, 105–6
defined, 23
linked to curriculum, 29, 30
and participant relationships, 24–25
hermeneutics
in action research project, 30, 39,
141
and border pedagogy, 19
conservative, 23, 24
and education, 27–30
moderate, 24–25
versus modernist position, 136–37
overview, 20–23
radical, 25–26
See also action research;
hermeneutic circle
"Hermeneutics, General Studies and
Teaching" (Rorty), 28
Hirsch, E. D., 23
Hobsbawm, Eric, 54, 90, 91, 96
Hodgetts, A. B.
on Canadian identity in schools, 82
on futility of national identity
search, 83, 84, 101, 131
on identity in relation to problems,
111–12
What History? What Heritage? , 71
Hoffman, Diane, 50, 115, 122, 126
Hollins, Etta R., 50
Houtekamer, Tweela, 89
Howard, R. J., 23
Hubbell, Jay, 90
Hutcheon, Linda, 112
Huyssen, Andreas, 96, 97
hypertrophy, 85

I
identity as ambiguity, 103–6
See also absurdism; ambiguity of
classroom teachers; bilingualism;
national identity
identity webs, 127–28, 130
Ignatieff, Michael, 39, 40, 43, 44, 46,
112

Studies in the Postmodern Theory of Education

General Editors
Joe L. Kincheloe & Shirley R. Steinberg

Counterpoints publishes the most compelling and imaginative books being written in education today. Grounded on the theoretical advances in criticalism, feminism, and postmodernism in the last two decades of the twentieth century, Counterpoints engages the meaning of these innovations in various forms of educational expression. Committed to the proposition that theoretical literature should be accessible to a variety of audiences, the series insists that its authors avoid esoteric and jargonistic languages that transform educational scholarship into an elite discourse for the initiated. Scholarly work matters only to the degree it affects consciousness and practice at multiple sites. Counterpoints' editorial policy is based on these principles and the ability of scholars to break new ground, to open new conversations, to go where educators have never gone before.

For additional information about this series or for the submission of manuscripts, please contact:

> Joe L. Kincheloe & Shirley R. Steinberg
> c/o Peter Lang Publishing, Inc.
> 275 Seventh Avenue, 28th floor
> New York, New York 10001

To order other books in this series, please contact our Customer Service Department:

> (800) 770-LANG (within the U.S.)
> (212) 647-7706 (outside the U.S.)
> (212) 647-7707 FAX

Or browse online by series:

> www.peterlangusa.com